The Promise

by

Hal Bynum

Copyright © 2002 by Hal Bynum

All rights reserved. No part of this book may be reproduced or transmitted in any form or by any means, electronic, or mechanical, including photo-copying, recording, or by any information storage and retrieval system, without the permission in writing from the publisher, except by reviewers who may quote brief passages in their reviews.

Published by
Beauregard Records and Books,
P.O. Box 158397,
Nashville, TN
37215-8397

Printed in the United States of America

Design by Tyler McGhee, The Eleazar Group

ISBN 0-9719501-0-5

First Edition

Table of Contents

Dedication vii
Acknowledgements ix
A Parable About Mirrors 1
Red Shoes, 1941 2
The Promise 4
Exodus, 1946 6
Tom Bynum 9
Bob Montgomery's Office, 1974 12
Stop Records, 1968 14
If I Could Do Anything I Wanted To 18
Hank Williams and His Drifting Cowboys 19
The Old, Old House 23
I Turned Your Picture to the Wall 24
A Pact with Violence 25
Papa Was a Good Man 30
Rosa's Western Club, 1955 31
The Comeback 33
"Kid" 35
There Ain't No Good Chain Gang 39
The Red Quarter, 1975 40
Forgiveness 41
Christopher 42
Last Summer 47
"Lucille" 49
Song of the Overseas Birds 52
Fair Park Auditorium, 1956 54
Pictures 55
An Old Man's Prayer 66
The World's Greatest Fiddle Player 68
Russell C. Skidmore, Coal Miner and Soldier, Retired 72
So Little of God and So Much Of The Other 74

Chuck Howard, 1969	75
Everything's Different Now	78
At a Restaurant with Christopher	80
A Lover's Prayer	82
St. Louis, 1977 – Ft. Worth, 1954	84
Two Women	87
Full Circle	89
Love at First Sight and Forever	91
A Leap of Understanding	93
Johnny Dollar and the Meat Cleaver	95
After a Scrape	97
Christmas Party, 1974	98
Meeting in Reno	99
Marigold, 1981	101
The Strange Disappearance of Lyla	105
Chuck Howard, 1983	106
The Miracle	110
Ray Price, 1972	111
Table Manners	120
Home	121
Apologia	123
We Had It All Figgered Out	125
I Wanta Be	127
Sugar	129
Eventide	131
Tryin' to Lose Weight	132
"Chains, Chains, Shackles and Chains"	134
Doodads and Trinkets	139
"Bud"	140
Fathers and Sons	144
The Change (A Kind of a Christmas Carol)	146
There'll Be Love	148
Winter Beaches	149

For Rebecca

Acknowledgements

I want to thank some people whose help has been necessary. People to whom I feel extremely grateful. People like Joey Reynolds at WOR in New York City for making us known nationally; Bill Mack, now of XM satellite radio; Rusty Walker and Phil Hunt Doyle of Rusty Walker Productions; Bill Cody, Kyle Cantrell, John Malone, Eddie Stubbs, Keith Bilbrey and all the wonderful workers at WSM; and to Pete Fisher, Jimmy Dickens and all the great ones at the Opry – THANK YOU!

I want to thank my longsuffering friends, Frankie Miller and Earl Hart of the Ft. Worth mafia, and Billy Don Burns and Sorrels Pickard, both of whom have saved me, a time or two; and Frances Preston, my pal and protector.

Of course I want to thank my long time great friend and manager, Merle Kilgore, who has tirelessly and courageously guided my career for years. And of course, David Hoffner, the arranger and co-producer of my new album, who always understands what I'm trying to do and then makes it happen.

And to my life's partner, who I am always writing about – the other half of me – Rebecca Bynum, without whom, nothing would get done.

And to all the others, everywhere,

Thanks,

Hal

Parable About Mirrors

In the evening when the work was done, the boy liked to sit on the front porch with his grandfather and try to see the world through the old man's eyes.

About an hour before sundown, the first team of mules pulled the first wagon even with the house and the driver called from the road,

"We're just movin' here. What kind of neighbors can we expect?"

The old man took some time examinin' the wagonload of furniture and the driver before he asked,

"What kinda folks was they where you're comin' from?"

The driver spat a long stream of tobacco spit and said,

"Dambdest bunch of people to wanta talk agin you and plot agin' you I ever saw. Not a decent one among 'em."

The old man nodded, "Yeah, well that's the way you'll find them here."

Before long, the second wagon with the second family pulled up in front of the house and the second driver asked the same question.

"What kind of people are we gonna have for neighbors?"

Again the old man asked,

"How was they whur you come from?"

The second driver shook his head sadly,

"The finest people you can imagine. Always ready to pitch in and help out. We hated to leave on their account."

The old man nodded,

"Yeah, well that's the way you'll find them here."

Before the last wagon was out of sight, the boy's mother called from inside the house that their supper was ready. The old man stood up, checked his pocket watch to see what time he
was quitting, and then followed the boy into the house.

(Hal Bynum, Andite Invasion/BMI From the Album, If I Could Do Anything, 1998)

Red Shoes, 1941

Hal's dad was a good farmer, but he had the reputation of being a drunk and this made it hard for him to rent land. Every so often they would get put off a place and wouldn't have another one to go to, and when this happened they would have to find a house to rent and live off the money his mother made teaching school.

These were the hard years for his Dad, sitting in winter kitchens drinking coffee and listening to the wind moan around the corner of the house, stunned by defeat and ashamed of that part of himself that liked it.

They moved to the Gellispie house in the fall. The old man who had owned the farm had died that year and the old lady had gone to live with their daughter in town. A neighbor was working the place and no one needed the house.

There were giant trees all around the little farmhouse and in the fall when the leaves were still on the trees, it was dark in the house.

One night it was raining and the woman and the two children were sitting at the round eating table, all three of them holding books toward the kerosene lamp in the center of the table.

In the next room Hal's father was lying across a white painted iron bedstead in his underwear. Every now and then he would vomit loudly onto the newspapers his mother had spread around the bed.

Mary Jo was using the turmoil to campaign for a new pair of red shoes. Long ago she had learned how to control their mother and whenever their father faltered, she took the helm.

"I'm ashamed to ride the bus in those old shoes, much less wear them to a party. You've gone to all that trouble to make me that beautiful red dress and now he won't let me have the shoes that match it. We can't ever have anything because of the way he spends all the money you make on whiskey. It's not his money anyway. He never makes any money."

Mary Jo's voice was cautious and reasonable as she leaned a little closer to the lamp, her eyes shining like a wolf's eyes moving up to a campfire. She had started looking in mirrors and worrying about her appearance lately.

"Oh I know it Darling. Every time we get hold of a little money so that we can have a few decent things and live like other people he—"

"He doesn't want me to have any fun. He's miserable and he wants us all to be."

The room was suddenly drenched with white light and then a crash of thunder shook the house and rolled off into the vast blackness of the Texas night.

Hal kept trying to read the library book named "Down the River Road." It was about some kids working together to make money with a donkey and a cart. The drawings had palm trees in them and Hal wondered where the kids lived.

Mary Jo was doodling on one of her book covers with a fountain pen. It was a cut-on-the-line-and-spit-on-the-sticky-stuff brown paper cover with a Phillips 66 advertisement in green ink. Mary Jo was making two more sixes to form four sixes in a row.

"People will laugh at me if I wear those same old brown school shoes I wear everyday."

A crafty look came over Mary Jo's face then and she was quiet for a moment. "You should have heard them laughing when he came to school to get us the other day and passed out in the car. They were laughing at him, but they were laughing at Harold and me too."

Her mother looked sick, and Hal suddenly saw again the picture of his father sprawled asleep in the car, his mouth open and his head cocked at a crazy angle.

Mary Jo started crying and turned up the wick on the lamp so their mother could see the tears.

"You don't care if they laugh at us or not! You promised me you'd quit him the next time he got drunk! You know how bad I've wanted those shoes!"

The woman was crying now too, and she said, "Oh Darling, I know it. It's not right. I'm not going to let—"

Suddenly they heard the creak of the bedsprings in the next room and then the sound of the man's knees on the newspapers.

"God! Can you hear me?!!"

All three of their heads turned toward the bedroom, their mouths open with horror.

"Please! Listen! Please, give Mary Jo them goddamn shoes so I can get some sleep! And make sure they're red! And make 'em—" He paused then and they heard him turn toward them in the dark room, "—what size you wear Mary Jo?"

Just then the figure of the man kneeling beside the bed was illuminated and transfigured by white light an instant before the house shook with thunder.

The woman screamed and ran to slam the bedroom door. When she came back to the table she put her face in her hands and began to sob. The only other sound was the rain falling from the eaves of the old farmhouse.

The Promise

You know Darlin, I've been wantin' to talk to you about sump'm for a long time an I couldn't quite figger out how to go about it.

You're a happy person an a joyful person an we laugh an kid around an enjoy each other all the time, but once in awhile I see a look of fear, or dread, come into your eyes and I've finally realized what that look means.

It means ... you're afraid of me gittin' interested in somebody else ... an you, losin' me.

I want you to know, once an fer all, an I'll repeat it however many times you need to hear it, that you couldn't never lose me. There won't ever be a time when I won't choose you, above all others. There won't ever be a mornin' when I don't wake up lovin' you more than I did the day before.

All kinds of things'll change, but that's not one of 'em. You've got to realize that.

Over the years, I'd gotten tired of people havin' to forgive me, and I'd begun to change, a little at a time; and by the time we met, I was ready to be honest with a woman, and to make you a full partner in my life.

From the first, you opened your heart to me and allowed yourself to be vulnerable and I knew I couldn't ever hurt you or allow anything else to hurt you, if I could help it.

Back before we got together, somebody had betrayed you ... an that leaves a scar an a sore place ... an it takes a long time for sump'm like that to heal. I guess there's probaly some little place in the back of your mind that flinches when it comes time to trust.

But you need to know that since we've been together, ever day of my life has been wonderful.

Before I met you my whole life had been empty an lonely. You think I'd want to go back to that? You're in ever thought I thaink. If it's sump'm good, I cain't wait to tell you about it, to share it with you.

You thaink I'd do some silliness with somebody else an take a chance on losin' what we have? An you'd know immediately by the different way I acted toward you, by the way I looked at you. I'd never hurt you like that.

You might could forgive me, but I couldn't forgive myself. We wouldn't ever be the same. It'd trivialize what we have, an what we are together.

You don't ever have to worry about anythaing like that.

I won't ever be untrue to you.

(Hal Bynum, Andite Invasion/BMI From the Album, The Promise, 2002)

Exodus 1946

An empty and forlorn West Texas childhood;
Ringlin' Brothers Circus,
Harley Sadler's tent show,
A ride on a train through the
black Texas night when Mama's daddy died
like little colored glass jewels
in a sandy wasteland of endless days
The wind moanin' around the corner of the house

People drawn out of the country,
drawn toward the town, the way
a Hills Brothers coffee poultice
draws the puss out of a sore,
the way a mustard plaster draws a chest cough,
drawn out of the farmland by the
weak pulsing electric lights
of the little country towns.
The slow pulsin' pull of the
lights we thought were bright.
A waitress in a greasy spoon cafe,
a coke sign on the side of the
building, in the alley there's a fight.
The Dairy Queen's closed for the winter
the picture show's closed for the night.

Drawn out of the wasteland of
tumbleweeds, bad health and sorrow,
Lamplights behind faded curtains,
flickerin' and going out,
The slow, rattlin' movement toward the township.
Rent paid, or owed, for a house on the edge of town
a job promised in November,
burning hulls at the cotton gin.

Rooster got a job drivin' the school bus,
Leeland's been drunk since he come back from the war
Grandma's finally got on the old age pension
Suzanne paid cold cash for a car
Hershel gave up his job
at the court house
Him an his whole family moved
to Dallis. They say he's
sellin' wheat futures an livin'
in a house on Mockin' Bird Lane
High Dollar, High Dollar!
They shut down the school at
Pleasant Hill and the train don't run
to Cobleswitch anymore.
I seen three John Deer tractors
sold at an auction with
go-devils, cultivators an all.

There's a movement from the
farm to the county seat -
People livin' on borrowed
money an makin' bad decisions,
I heard Marvin Hightower say,
"My wife'll spend money at the beauty parlor
when there ain't no meat nor whiskey in the house."
Said he'd rather be back in the country,
readin' the paper by a coal oil lamp

There ain't enough people livin
at Whitbarrel to support the
Preacher anymore. He loaded
everthing they owned, which
wadn't much, on a truck
and moved to East Texas.

I know a fellow says he can
git me a job workin' at
Swift's or Armour's on the north side
of Fort Worth. I don't know if
I could stand slaughterin' hogs
day in and day out. They say
once you work there you won't
never eat another bite of sausage.
Everbody around here seems to be
goin' somewhere else, to do
sumpm' different - - - -

Nothin's like it was before the war.

Tom Bynum

Tom Bynum was an animal. Once Hal understood that about his grandfather, everything fell into place. There was no way he could have been socialized. You could see it in his sisters, too. They had that wary, inward look, just this side of sullen.

Hal was kind of a jake-legged, shade tree historian, and when he was a boy he would sit for hours, looking at old discolored photographs of his ancestors. They were usually grouped on and around the front porches of a series of old deteriorating farmhouses.

His mother's family were all tall, sandy haired, distinguished looking people with blue eyes and aquiline noses, a nervous and restless people.

Tom Bynum was short and powerfully build, with long thick arms that hung halfway to his knees. He had an aversion to talking and to learning, and during his lifetime he was almost totally successful in avoiding both.

He was famous in central Texas as a mule-skinner and horse breaker, but was more widely known for bare-knuckle fighting. Men would travel from other parts of Texas to try him, and sometimes they would fight all day in a pasture, taking timeout for a lunch under the black jack and cottonwood trees. He was a very serious man, to whom humor was foreign. The only time anyone remembered him laughing was once when four drunken soldiers from Fort Hood surrounded him in front of the wagon yard in Gatesville and told him they were going to "whip his ass."

Tom was a mule-skinner in Coryell County for many years, freighting store goods, grain and timber, but after fighting, he was best known for being able to break horses and mules that everyone else had given up on.

When a man tries and fails to break a horse or a mule, he creates a monster, a creature full of treachery and defiance, breathing hate and animosity, completely worthless as a beast of burden.

This was the kind of animal Tom Bynum liked to get a hold of. When he was finished with them, they were as docile and dependable as the old mares people keep for their children to ride.

He had neither the intelligence nor the inclination to acquire land or amass money, and since he was a periodic drunk, there were many times when the family had to live on corn cakes and molasses and go to school without decent clothes.

He was working on the Wallace ranch, making a dollar a day, working eighteen hours a day, seven days a week, grubbing trees and feeding livestock, when word came from Baylor County, out in West Texas, that there was a job for him, and a job for his wife, cooking for the Howe Brothers ranch.

The woman saw a chance to feed what was left of the children (four had died and two of the girls had run off with a vaudeville show) and a chance to send one of them, the girl, to business school. She took the bull by the horns, so to speak. She hooked up the team, drove to old man Lige Wallace's ranch and told him Tom was quitting. When she got back home, she and the boy and girl loaded everything they had into a covered wagon, then argued, cajoled and begged the aging gladiator onto the flat board seat and then pulled out, heading west, the beautiful, prematurely white haired woman driving, for Tom refused to drive the mules, help make camp, or fry the side meat and potatoes at night. He had the animal's disinclination to abandon the accustomed trotting paths, watering holes, and game stalking places of his youth. He feared neither man nor beast, but the unknown immobilized him.

When Tom Bynum was ninety years old, and the great barrel chest and the monstrous hands were loosely covered with parchment-like skin and the deep, booming, seldom used voice had become a controlled rattle, Hal and his drinking friend, Earl Hart drove out to the rest home on Pennsylvania Avenue in Fort Worth to visit the old man on a Sunday afternoon.

Earl tried valiantly to start a conversation. "Mr. Bynum, did you ever have a horse run away with you?"

The old eyes stared with pity at the young men, softened by civilization and made frivolous and foolish by a world which provided no physical challenges.

"I had some that run with me. I didn't have any that run away."

The old man sat in silent and effortless dignity, neither perceiving nor ignoring the youngsters. Finally, Earl made another sally.

"Mr. Bynum, you were born during the Civil War, you grew up when this country was still the frontier. You've lived to see jet planes and the atom bomb. Of all you've seen, what has made the biggest impression on you?"

For a time there was no indication that he had heard the elaborate and pretentious question, but then a spark of interest showed in the watery blue eyes.

"Well, I'll tell you, the Goddamndest thing I ever saw was one time when I was freightin' for old man Hobin. I come up on this steer layin' dead and I thinks, 'What in the world's happened to this steer?' There wadn' a mark on him anywhere and if he'd been struck by lightnin', you coulda smelt it and seen where it scorched him. I gets down off my wagon and gives him a goin' over and I cain't find a thing wrong with him. Finally,——— I thinks to look in his mouth and I be Goddamned if he hadn' swallowed a lightnin' rod and choked his self to death."

The Bull Durham roll your-own had burned almost down to the brown stained fingers and he put it out in the ashtray.

"I never could cipher out what that lightnin' rod was doin' off out in the middle of nowhere or what got into that steer to want to eat it."

At the time, the story had meant nothing more to Hal than a demonstration of the old man's lack of a sense of history, but years later, he would compare the steer to the dead leopard in "The Snows of Kilimanjaro."

Like Hemingway, Tom Bynum had never discovered any reality higher than the physical world.

When Hal had come to Nashville and found the town locked up politically, his old feelings of isolation and helplessness had returned and the cornered animal came out when he drank. He would drink whiskey and go crazy, tearing up offices and terrorizing people.

He had brought Tom Bynum's act to Nashville and it was a show-stopper, to say the least.

Bob Montgomery's Office, 1974

Hal hated to wait in outer offices. In those days he didn't care much for record producers, and when the receptionist called to announce his presence, if the producer didn't say, "Tell him to come on in," Hal would usually open the door and go in anyway. The receptionist would say something like, "Wait! You can't—" but by then he would close the door in her face, turn toward the producer and whoever had an appointment with him, give them his most disarming smile and say, "Howdy, Howdy!"

He would roll his humor on them: the producer would start laughing first and before long, in spite of himself the man whose appointment he was interrupting would join in.

One afternoon about four o'clock, he entered Bob Montgomery's office, back when it was across from Columbia. Bob was producing Bobby Goldsboro at the time and they owned a publishing company together.

Hal had started for Montgomery's office and the secretary, Rose, had said, "Hal! He's got someone with him. I'll tell him you're here." When she put the phone down she said, "He says for you to have a seat."

Hal glanced around the room. There were three more people waiting.

"They all waitin' fer Bob?"

The secretary nodded.

Hal shrugged, "OK-that's alright."

Rose sighed with relief as he walked toward an easy chair. Hal sat his drink of whiskey on a coffee table, casually stripped off all his clothes, selected a magazine from the table and sat down, beginning to flip through the pages of "U.S. News and World Report," buck naked.

Hal appeared to be engrossed in the magazine but he could see Rose in his peripheral vision. She came around her desk slipping and sliding in her stocking feet, heading for Bob's office. If she had had her high heels on she might have been injured as she hurled herself forward, her face slack with shock.

In a moment, Bob's head and shoulders protruded from the doorway. His eyes went wide and his mouth came open. He ran to the vicinity of Hal's chair and began hurriedly to gather up the discarded clothing, saying, "Hal! Hal!"

Hal glanced up from the magazine. "Bob. How you doin', son?"

The producer held all of the clothes and boots between his left arm and his body, and with the other, he seized Hal's bicep, "Hal! Come in here, come in my office!"

Hal reluctantly laid the periodical on the table, picked up his drink and followed Bob into the inner office, never looking at the other people.

Montgomery closed the door, locked it and turned to stare at Hal, still holding the clothes and boots. A young fellow was sitting in a chair holding a guitar, unable to believe what he was seeing.

Hal strode across, lifted the guitar from his hands and turned toward Bob, sliding his bare ass onto a corner of the glass topped desk. He hit a "D" chord.

"Bob, I appreciate you making time for me. This thing is a monster for Goldsboro. Biggern' 'Honey.'"

He began to sing and play.

Stop Records, 1968

Hal pulled up and parked across the street from Stop records. He sat in the car - studying the white two-story building. The only marking was an enlarged version of the traffic sign. He took a deep breath, crawled out of the little Plymouth Valiant that was packed full of everything he owned, and walked across the street, his heart pounding. It was the moment he had dreaded and delayed for years, the time when he would knock on the door of a Nashville publisher and present himself as a candidate to become a viable, working part of the voluble viscous lava-like flow of heart music that erupted in this southern town and flowed inexorably into every village and hamlet in the land.

He had known for a long time that he needed to do it, if he was ever going to do it, but he had put it off, continuing to work as a welfare social worker in New Mexico, spending all the time he could with his son, Scott Thomas, and pitching songs to the country singers who came through Albuquerque.

His songs were playing everywhere and it was time to make the move, but still he delayed. Finally fate, or something, insinuated its hand into the panorama of human events and he was arrested while driving drunk. Since there was a car wreck involved, they took him to the jail section of the county hospital and during the night he managed to escape.

The next day, Hal was on the front page of the newspaper and his career as a welfare caseworker was finished. He had headed for Nashville, but stopped off in Fort Worth and applied for a job working in the General Dynamics aircraft factory. To his surprise, he was hired, and so he worked on the night shift, riding a bicycle delivering parts and writing songs in his head. His old friend Frankie Miller immediately recorded two of them for Stop Records. One of them, "Pain," was released and started playing strongly in Texas.

Hal would have been content to stay in Fort Worth, writing and pitching songs to the big recording artists who worked Panther Hall on weekends, but he was caught drinking on the job and fired. About the same time, the finance company who owned his car found him and attempted to repossess the little Plymouth. He escaped from them twice, after wild, death defying pursuits, but he realized that sooner or later they would trap him and the car would be gone and he would be afoot. So, he decided to move to Laredo where his friend, Homer Logan, was working. He loaded-up his guitar and clothes and started for Laredo, drunk on wine. Somewhere along the road he went into a blackout and when he came to, he was on the outskirts of Nashville, the floorboards full of empty bottles and half-eaten hamburgers.

That autumn morning he had drunk enough of the remaining wine to steady his nerves, shaved, changed shirts and found Stop Records' address in a phone book.

As he pushed the door open, he saw Tommy Hill sitting at a desk on the right end of the room. Tommy didn't recognize him at first. They had met when Tommy was producing Frankie Miller at Starday. Hal had traveled with Frankie during the time right after "Blackland Farmer" had been rediscovered and had quickly become a pop hit.

"What are you doing in Nashville?" Tommy asked politely, struggling to keep his eyes from wandering to the paperwork on his desk. He had not laid down his pencil.

Hal told him he was looking for a job as a staff-writer for a publishing house. He mentioned that he had written "Pain." Tommy had grown a little mustache.

"I don't think Pete would even consider hiring another writer. We've got a full roster here." He glanced down at the paperwork. "You might try Tree or Hill and Range or one of the big outfits. Window is still a small operation."

Tommy worked for Pete Drake, a steel player who had worked recording sessions for years and had recently recorded a hit instrumental, "Forever." He owned Window music and quietly and carefully hawked songs to the artists who hired him for sessions. He had started his own label as an outlet for his publishing catalog, hiring Tommy Hill away from Starday and developing a staff of writers.

"You mentioned the Frankie Miller record. I know it's gettin' some airplay in Texas, couple of markets, but the other side is taking off everywhere else. We're trying to get the Texas jocks to go with us on the thing. The worst thing you can have happen is to get a split record. If that happens you're dead."

Frankie had warned Hal that if he didn't give Pete the publishing on "Pain," Pete would try to turn the record over. He owned the publishing on the other side and the radio performance money was the main thing. Hal knew there was no use telling him how heavily it was being played in Texas and remind him that if it didn't break out in Texas, it wouldn't break out at all.

Tommy was writing on pages and turning them over now, his head bent over the desk. Hal had stood up to leave when Chuck Howard exploded through the door.

"Tom, my boy, they've decided to screw us. To bend us over and with savage aforethought,..." Chuck broke into a boyish grin, "I read that somewhere, 'savage aforethought.'" He was enjoying himself. The chuckle stopped and he dropped the big booming voice down into the scrawny chest and bellowed, "Distributors! Goddamn Distributors! I wish I had 'em all by the —Cousin!" Hal had taken off his hat so Chuck would recognize him. Chuck called everybody cousin. "Cousin, what in the world are you doin'?!" He pulled Hal from the chair and embraced him. "What happened to the beard? I didn't know you for a minute!"

Hal realized that no one had spoken but Chuck since he had burst in. His personality completely filled the room. "Aw, I had a couple of straight jobs. I had ta shave it off."

"What 'r you doin'? Did you ever get loose from Pamper?" Chuck had on a powder blue three-piece suit with his dark blue shirt collar open above his suit jacket. When Hal nodded, Chuck widened his eyes and shouted, "How'd you do it, how'd you get loose from that old man?!"

Hal grinned ruefully and held up four fingers on his right hand.

Chuck screamed with laughter, "Tommy look at that!" Tommy was watching dispassionately. He had put down the pencil when Chuck came in, giving up on the paperwork. Chuck grabbed Tommy by the shoulder and howled, "Get it? Four years! Hal Smith held his feet to the fire for the full four years!"

"I out-lived the son of a bitch." Hal didn't want to get into all that.

Chuck grabbed Tommy's shoulder and pointed to Hal, "This man is funny. God, he's funny!" He looked at Tommy and held up four fingers on his right hand and did the laugh again. Tears were coming out of his eyes now and he looked at Hal and shook his head, "Cousin, you are so funny! I've missed you. You're the only one that can make me laugh."

Chuck gave Tommy a mock sideways scathing look and said, "I have to pull these bastards like cotton sacks."

Tommy finally smiled a little bit, then Chuck continued, "Who are you writin' for?"

"Nobody. I just came by here to see if I could—"

"Son! You're free? You haven't signed with anybody yet?" Chuck bent his knees slightly, pointed to Hal with his right hand and stretched the other hand out to Tommy, imploring him, "Tommy! You've gotta sign this man! He's a great writer! A great writer! I'm tellin' you, I've heard his stuff and it's great! A lot of big cuts. Price, George Jones, on and on. Sign the man!"

Hal had never had a Price cut.

The little man at the table shook his head, "I was just tellin' him, Chuck, Pete told me that—"

"Aw yeah, you're right. He didn't get that money." Chuck was suddenly in deep thought. He came out of it quickly and turned to Hal, saying confidentially, "He's gonna have to sue some people for some money an' he's broke right now. I'd forgot." He turned to Tommy, violently in motion again, "Who's hiring writers?" he demanded. "This man's a hell of a writer an' he needs to get rollin'."

Tommy was still looking peeved at Chuck for revealing family secrets.

"Well, I don't know Chuck, maybe Mary Reeves, she's always—"

"Yeah! Yeah! Clarence Selman. They're throwing money around like it was goin' outta style! That's it! Com'on, I can turn that trick for you!" He darted toward the door, making a rapid repeated gesture with his hand, signaling Hal to follow, "Com'on, Com'on!"

* * *

The next morning Hal met with Clarence at Mary Reeves' office in Madison and got the job. It wasn't exactly like Chuck had described. Clarence spent most of the interview describing how much money they had spent on writers and how little had come of it. Apparently, the answer was no. Hal felt the old left out feeling. He had about six dollars in his pocket, no place to sleep, it was winter and it was raining. The feeling turned to anger, which was distributed evenly between Chuck and the slow-drawling, chain smoking man behind the desk. Hal had offered him the publishing on "Pain" and several as yet unrecorded songs he had written in Forth Worth, but Clarence had not been impressed.

As Hal got up to leave he said, "Ya'll have got the publishing on a song of mine. It's been here several years and you haven't even got a record on it. I'd like to get it back."

Clarence looked bored and tired, "Really, what's the name of it?"

"Nobody's Fool."

Clarence froze, his eyes suddenly penetrating and alert. "Nobody's Fool, a pretty ballad?"

"Yeah. It might help me get a deal somewhere."

Clarence continued to stare at Hal for a few seconds, "Excuse me. I've gotta have a word with Mary."

He came back shortly and told Hal that he had Jim Reeves' next single.

Shortly before he was killed in an airplane crash, Jim had cut a demonstration record of the ballad, hoping Johnny Cash or Jimmy Dickens would cut it. The demo Hal had given him had been out of meter and Reeves, being a perfectionist, had re-recorded it himself. He had had almost nothing in the can at the time of his death and R.C.A. had mastered the demo, dubbing in violins, and scheduled it for his next single release. He was hotter now than he had been when he was alive.

Since Mary knew she would recoup her money from "Nobody's Fool," whether Hal turned out to be a productive writer or not, she gave him a six month contract at fifty dollars a week and Clarence began demoing the songs Hal had brought to Nashville and the ones he had written while he was working nights in a gas station on Dickerson Road.

Chuck had got him started.

If I Could Do Anything I Wanted To

If I could do anything I wanted to, I'd sit on a stool with an old guitar that had a good ring to it, and I'd sing in a good clear voice, a lot better'n mine, but not too good cause I'd want em to listen to the song and not the singer. And I'd sing out in the open, in some valley where the sound would carry a long, long way. I'd do it in the evenin' so people could come out of their houses and listen after the day's work was done. An I'd sing about love, and I'd sing about people, an I'd sing about rivers and children in little dresses and britches, pullin' wagons with other kids in 'em an dogs runnin' around 'em an barkin'.

I'd sing about happy smiles on children's faces - an I'd sing about men workin' in coal mines way down under the ground, an about old folks with bodies that know how to work, but can't do it anymore.

I'd sing about sunrises and sunsets an cold, raw winds that sweep across the land, an birthdays, and reunions, an a pretty ring on a young woman's hand. I'd tell about brave voices in church houses, an laughter and gossip on phone lines. I'd sing about the smell of coffee in the mornin' an food fryin' in a pan - an men workin' on the family car, tryin' to get it runnin' again.

An when I knew everybody was out on their porch an listenin', when the song had reached every ear, I'd start singin' about the Father, an kindness, an the way love feels when it replaces the darkness in a heart. I'd tell how forgiveness brings freedom, an I'd play softly so the words could sink in.

I'd sing 'em a song about Jesus, about glory an beauty an crowds listenin' to mercy with their feet in the hot desert sand. I'd tell about life on other planets where wars and famine are long gone, where the competition is for service, an every eye sees the light.

Then I'd stop singin' an playin' - an I'd listen to the sound of millions of voices singin' softly an hummin', a harmonious hymn from hearts touched by God. An when the last pink border of twilight faded from the sky in the west, - I'd put away my guitar an be filled with feelings of thanksgiving, 'cause I was born to write a love song. That's what I'd do, if I could do anything I wanted to.

(Hal Bynum, Andite Invasion/BMI From the Albums, *If I Could Do Anything*, 1998 and *It's My Time*, 1995)

Hank Williams and His Drifting Cowboys

Hal sat on the couch in his study on the top floor of the old house on Cedar Lane, studying the country music charts in Billboard Magazine.

"What a bunch of shit," he said aloud, dropping the magazine in his lap. He began to stare through the window and think of the records he had heard on the radio in 1953. It was called hillbilly music back then and it had an undiluted power and appeal that was lacking in its modern counterpart.

That year he and his dad had been farming a half section of new-broken ground near Denver City, near the New Mexico line. The sandy hills and arroyos had been stripped of sage brush and post oak shinery by bulldozers. The irrigation pumps pulled an eight-inch stream from the water table far below and forced it through a sprinkler system to wet the sand dunes and grow cotton and maize. In the summer, giant thunderheads would pile up and move in from the east. A hot, dry wind would begin to move to meet them, drying and moving the sand along the cotton rows, burning the plants with static electricity. The tiny people would watch the approach of the beautiful high piled white clouds with dread, knowing they might not have a crop when the dark bottomed mass moved on over to deposit it's load of life-giving water on the farmland around Clovis and Portales.

The farmers would move the sprinklers as quickly as possible over the sand, followed by a tractor pulling a stalk-cutter to break the soil into clods so it would take longer for the lethal winds to dry it and set it moving again.

Hal would drive the tractor or carry pipe with the Mexicans seven days a week, but on Wednesday afternoons he would shower and put on the white navy uniform he wore to the Naval Reserve meetings in Lubbock.

As soon as he got in the car, he would turn the dial to a Lovington, New Mexico station that played hillbilly music and listen until he was past Denver City, then switch back and forth between the little station in Seagraves and the one in Seminole until he could catch KDAV's signal. KDAV was an all hillbilly music station in Lubbock and it was Hal's favorite.

The summer before he began college at Texas Tech, in Lubbock, which was the summer of 1953, he would drive the big Buick down the narrow two lane blacktop highway, passing pick-up trucks with gasoline drums in the back, listening to the radio, hurtling toward a mirage a mile and a half down the road that never came closer.

Occasionally, the growl of an irrigation well would drift in through the open window and he would glance into the field to see a man in a straw hat working with a spade or setting plastic tubes in cotton rows, but his mind was only aware of the music.

The fiddles and steel guitars wove a backdrop for the little scenes of human drama recounted by the nasal sounding hill voices of the country singers. Each song was a story, a brief glimpse of a life motivated and ruled by some emotion, whether it was love, anguish, despair or the fleeting feeling of transient happiness.

He heard the Davis sisters singing "I've Forgot More," Hank Locklin singing "Let Me Be The One," Eddy Arnold's record of "Condemned Without Trial," Slim Willet's recording of "Don't Let The Stars Get in Your Eyes," and each one gave him the warm-glow feeling of excitement that nothing else could bring him until he began to drink beer a year or so later.

He hadn't been able to fit into his family when he was a child and when he hadn't been able to join the larger group he was confronted with in school, he began to shun groups and attempt to find comfort in isolating himself from the rejection he always encountered when he tried to become a joiner.

The sweet, cloying, self-sympathy of hillbilly music came through the airwaves to find him and he was not alone anymore.

If these records were a pre-taste of the euphoria of beer, Hank Williams' records were a double shot of Wild Turkey whiskey, injected directly into his blood stream. The powerful, driving, pain-filled voice of Hank Williams sent a thrill through his body and pulled him into a world he had never experienced before.

Hal knew nothing about Hank's personal life at the time, but after hearing his records on the radio, the feeling that he was a man lost in despair was inescapable. The sound of hopelessness in his voice could not have been cultivated or contrived. He was obviously a man who had been handled roughly and had been badly damaged by an uncaring world, a victim of unfortunate circumstances and unattainable love.

He was a loser who had made it all the way to the top, and it was inevitable that Hal would make Hank his hero. With no reluctance or hesitation, he joined the ranks of the lonely, self -pitying, young men who identified with Hank and made him their idol.

After Hank died in the back seat of a Cadillac limousine on New Year's morning of 1953, he dominated the airwaves to an extent he had never been able to accomplish during his lifetime. The sympathy he had cried out for was released by his premature death and it rolled across the world of country music like a tidal wave, too late for Hank to feel it or be affected by it.

At the time, Hal had no way of knowing what a threat this was to other performers. When their records were played, they were fill-ins and side-shows, aired only because the disk jockeys couldn't play hour after hour of Hank's music, although that would have been fine with the listeners. They were completely preoccupied with the sound and message he had created.

One of Hank's last releases was "I'll Never Get Out of This World Alive," and when he proved out his prophecy, it occurred to his fans that he really had been writing and singing about his life, and they began to thumb back through their memory, examining each song and weaving a legend out of the fabric of his life.

As the other singers worked auditoriums across the nation, they soon found that the only way to bring the audiences alive was to do one of Hank's songs. Suddenly the crowd's restless apathy would be gone and they would explode, like a flag had been brought on stage during wartime.

Years later, Frankie Miller told Hal a story about Ray Price. Price had been a friend and protégé of Hank's and had traveled with him and put up with his insane behavior when he was drunk, which was most of the time, during the last few years of his life.

That summer, Price was being backed by Hank's old band, "The Drifting Cowboys" and radio stations were coming down heavy on "Hank Williams' Drifting Cowboys" in order to pack the auditoriums and clubs where Price was playing.

Price was sitting in the back seat of a car parked in front of the club, shortly before time for him to go on, having a few drinks and passing the bottle back and forth between Frankie and the club owner, who were sitting in the front seat. The car radio was on and they would all stop talking and listen each time the station did a spot advertising Price's appearance.

After awhile, Price stopped talking and sat staring at the radio, his face expressionless. When the spot played again, he suddenly lurched forward, reaching over the car seat to snap the radio off. He lowered himself back into the seat again, took a swallow from the whiskey bottle and looked out the back window of the car for a few moments before he said softly, "To hell with Hank Williams and his Driftin' Cowboys!"

Hal sat on the couch and thought of how he had followed the lonely music through the barrooms and backstages of the land, living out an imitation of Hank's life, complete with booze, women and jails; ever true to the dream, unswerving and untiring in his belief that somewhere in the glittering world of hillbilly music there was a place for him.

Suddenly, the terrible struggle involved with making it to the top of a business for which he had absolutely no talent, came back to him; every recording artist he had cornered and forced to listen to his songs, every local band leader he had conned into making demo tapes of his songs, every disk jockey he had wrangled and threatened in order to get a pick-hit for his songs.

"Songs, songs, songs. What away for a grown man to make a living," he thought, trying not to think about the struggle that lay ahead of him in getting his career going again after the drunken rampage he had made on music row, wrecking offices, jerking and knocking people around and causing Charlie Pride to fire him as his staff writer, stopping the flow of the first serious money he had made after all these years.

He suddenly grabbed the Billboard magazine out of his lap and flung it across the room to where it bounced off the bookcase and lay open on the shag carpet.

He stared at it for awhile and then said with bitterness, "To hell with Hank Williams and his Driftin' Cowboys."

The Old, Old House

There's an old, old house that once was a mansion
On a hill overlooking the town
But time has left wreckage where once there was beauty
And soon the old house will tumble down

But when the leaves start to fall in autumn
And the rain starts to drip from the trees
There's an old, old man who walks through the garden
And his head is bowed in memory

They say he built the mansion because of a woman
They planned to be married in the fall
But her love withered in the last days of summer
And the house stood empty after all

But when the leaves start to fall in autumn
And the rain starts to drip from the trees
There's an old, old man who walks through the garden
And his head is bowed in memory

(Hal Bynum Glad Music/BMI From the Album It's My Time, 1995)

I Turned Your Picture To The Wall

I turned your picture to the wall this morning
I turned your picture to the wall
And soon, your old memory, it won't bother me at all
I turned your picture to the wall

I've been holding on with all my heart
But today I'm letting go
Of all the years and all the tears
That never made love grow
For a long, long time my love was blind
And I refused to see
That you and I, we both loved you
And no one cared for me

I turned your picture to the wall this morning
I turned your picture to the wall
And soon, your old memory, it won't bother me at all
I turned your picture to the wall

Your picture won't look down on me
The way you've always done
Every dream that mattered
You shattered one by one
That tender touch that meant so much
Grew hard and cold as stone
And even though I'm lonely
I'll be better off alone

I turned your picture to the wall this morning
I turned your picture to the wall
And soon, your old memory, it won't bother me at all
I turned your picture to the wall

I turned your picture to the wall

(Hal Bynum, Andite Invasion/BMI From the Album It's My Time 1995)

A Pact with Violence

It was 1979, late at night and Hal was about three-quarters drunk. His third wife, Virginia, was asleep. He had called Bill Henderson in Lubbock and they had been talking for over an hour. Hal had just finished telling him his theory about what was wrong with himself and why he couldn't quit drinking.

He could see Henderson lying in bed listening patiently, probably with the light out so his wife could sleep.

"Bynum, you've grown up and read a lot of books and decided to start thinking like one of them hippies that are always analyzin' life and looking for a reason to feel defeated, so they can give up. You say the reason you can't quit drinkin' is fear. Let me tell you something Bynum, I've known you since you was a kid in school. I've known you off an on ever since. I give you a job when you came out of the Navy. I knew all along you'd git to the top of whatever business you got into. It wadn' no surprise to me the night I saw Roy Clark give you that award on network T.V. It may have surprised a lot of people, but not me. I'd seen you fight too many times. I taught you to fight. You can say whatever you want to about fear, but I'll tell you somethin'; you ain't NEVER been afraid of no son of a bitch in your life!"

Even as drunk as Hal was, he knew he couldn't explain what he meant. Henderson thought if you were afraid, you were afraid of somebody. He hadn't had that problem anymore than Henderson had. His fear had always been of failure: of not being able to cope with life when the moment of Truth arrived. He had a detached faith in God and the cosmos, but he had no confidence in himself. For most of his life, he didn't know that he was fearful. He thought he was angry. Then he had learned that anger, hate and resentment were all masks for fear.

He went into the kitchen of the mobile home and mixed another rum and coke. He shuffled over to the door, opening it and shoving it back against the outside of the trailer, he slowly and carefully sat down in the doorway, his feet on the iron steps and leaning the body cast against the doorway.

His broken neck hurt at all times, and the six metal bolts that were screwed through the flesh and into his skull were constantly painful. The marijuana smoke and the beer and liquor that he began consuming as soon as he got up in the morning could only do so much. His right arm, between the wrist and elbow, was smashed, but he paid little attention to it because the pain was not constant. The pain in his neck was like a phone that had been ringing without interruption for two months. A big outside telephone bell like they have at lumberyards.

Hal figured he was lucky that he had been torn up a lot in the past and had learned to deal with intense pain. He wouldn't take sedatives because he didn't want another addiction.

As much as he hated to lie, he lied to Virginia and everyone else about the pain. He knew it would depress them and they wouldn't want to be around him if they knew the pain was mortal and unceasing. Looking at him was bad enough, he could see that in their eyes. When George Jones had seen him, he had choked up with tears and fled from the room.

Another drunken car wreck, and this time it had almost canceled him.

Hal looked out at the field of soybeans, white-green in the moonlight. He rubbed the back of his neck with one hand and held the rum and coke with the other, reviewing his conversation with Henderson.

The year Hal was a junior in high school, the agriculture teacher had quit at mid-term and Henderson had taken the job. He had just retired from professional boxing, having been in the top ten in Ring Magazine for several years. He had fought everyone in his division who would fight him and some in the next heavier division, but had never been given a shot at the Championship. He was lightning fast and could knock you down with either hand; what they called a crowd pleaser. He had a manager who wasn't in with the right people, and one day Henderson finally realized that, although he could keep fighting and making money, they were never going to let him be champion. He was smart and he could look down the road and see the time coming when the hair trigger mechanism would slow down a fraction of a second and the legs wouldn't do what he told them to, and then he would be on the other end of the punishment. He had a clear head and he wanted to keep it that way.

Hal stood up, braced himself against the trailer and took a leak. He sat back down in the doorway and drank half the drink.

The best he could remember, he had taken agriculture so he wouldn't have to take Algebra II, or maybe it was a foreign language he was avoiding. Or maybe he had taken it so he could go on trips, he thought, rattling the ice in the glass.

His and Henderson's life-long friendship had begun the day he and another boy got into a fight during agriculture class.

For some reason, Hal had never been able to defend himself. He had a horror of hitting anyone with his fists. When another kid would hit him he would never fight back. All he could do was try to deflect the blows with his arms and hands and take whatever punishment was forthcoming.

Because of the way things had gone at home, he had a tremendous need for attention and approval, but the way he went about it, he got the attention, but not the approval. He had to go around entertaining everybody at all times, crowding to the center and taking control of every group, and even in those days, his scathing humor was abrasive enough to take the bark off a pine tree.

He would assault the leader of the group with his sarcasm and some of that person's followers would laugh nervously, others, farther from the center of the group, would laugh joyfully, and still others, who like Hal, couldn't fit into any group, would guffaw and hoot at the leader, hoping to see a fight.

If the fight came, Hal would be totally surprised and would, as always, refuse to defend himself. The whole process embarrassed the other kids and disrupted the comfortable little cliques they had settled into. They didn't like it, and they didn't like Hal.

The worst thing about it was, he couldn't keep from repeating the process over and over. The deep need that drove him was not a part of his consciousness, and he had no control over it.

The boy who picked a fight with him that morning was named Ansley and he had recently moved to town. His father followed the oil fields and the boy had been moved from town to town and from school to school so many times that he hadn't learned to make friends.

Apparently he had surveyed the scene and decided that the quickest way for him to win approval and become widely accepted was to pick a fight with Hal and thrash him soundly. From what he had heard and seen, there was no reason to think that Hal would fight back. He never had.

Hal was cutting a rusty fifty gallon oil drum in half with an acetylene torch and once when he stopped and pushed the dark goggles up on his forehead so he could adjust the flame, he noticed Ansley standing close by watching him and scowling. Just before he finished cutting the barrel in two, Ansley reached over, grabbed the torch out of his hand and ripped the goggles off his head.

"I need to use these."

Hal jumped up and grabbed hold of the torch and the boys wrestled briefly. The stockier built boy shoved Hal up against a hog feeder, dropped the torch, which was still burning and swung his right fist at Hal, hitting him on the left side of the head.

All the boys working in the shop dropped their tools and ran to form a circle around Hal and Ansley. Henderson broke through the circle and separated them.

He said calmly, "If you boys want to fight, you need to git out here in the middle of the floor where you won't be tearin' up feeders. Sammy, run out and git those eight ounce gloves out of the trunk of my car."

A cold stab of fear hit Hal's vitals. He knew what was coming. He wasn't afraid of what the boy could do to him, he had never gotten hurt in scuffles. What he dreaded was what the other boys and Henderson would think when he couldn't bring himself to hit Ansley. They would think he was a coward and he could never explain to them that he would rather get hurt than hurt someone else. They wouldn't believe it.

Hal's heart was pounding as Henderson tied the laces on his gloves. There was a label on the gloves that said "Everlast." When the gloves were laced and tied and the man had checked both pairs, he backed up and spread his arms and said, "All right, all you boys back up and give them room." He looked at Hal and Ansley. "Go to it."

The group sprang back to give the fighters room, screaming and hollering for blood, "Hit 'im Ansley! Give it to 'im Ansley! Knock his block off! You can do it!"

Ansley began to stalk forward, moving toward Hal, holding his hands side by side in front of him and moving his head back and forth behind the gloves.

The faces behind Ansley were a blur of hate and excitement. They made a noise like a pack of dogs.

Hal lurched forward and swung his right fist in a looping arc that struck Ansley in the nose and mouth. The boy's hands flew out and away from his face and he reeled backward, the blood spurting from his nose. Hal blundered after him, swinging like a windmill, missing twice and then connecting with another right. The blood splattered and he saw a look of terror on the boy's face.

Someone behind Hal shoved him hard in the small of his back and it catapulted him into Ansley, the top of his head hitting the already blood-covered face. The force of the blow knocked Ansley down and then Hal was standing above him, stomping him in the face.

Two or three sets of hands had a hold of Hal, pulling him back and away from the supine form. Everything that had happened since he had first punched the other boy was a blur to Hal. His body had done all of it without any instruction from him. When he had first seen the blood on Ansley's face, instead of feeling sorry for the boy, he had wanted to kill him.

The crowd pushed the fighters again and they came together swinging wildly. Hal was hit once in the face and once in the neck but he didn't even feel the punches.

Suddenly he had his left arm locked around Ansley's neck and was pounding his face with his right fist. Then they were out of the circle of boys and fighting among a bunch of barrels. They went down, one of the empty oil drums falling on top of them. Hal had Ansley's ear between his teeth and his mouth was full of the boy's blood. Ansley was screaming.

Henderson's voice cut through the sound of the snarling dog pack. "Let his ear go! Let go of his ear!"

The next thing Hal knew, they were standing face to face. Ansley's white dress shirt was torn and bloody.

"You boys shake hands now and be friends." Hal heard Henderson's voice from far off. Someone was taking his gloves off. He was so weak he could barely stand up and his lungs were on fire.

"Wayne, you take Ansley in the rest room and git him cleaned up. Go in and see if Coach Rattan's got a practice jersey he can wear the rest of the day. Bynum, you better go out to the fountain and rinse the blood out of your mouth. The rest of you boys git back to work. When you git done, I wanna see you in my office, Bynum."

When he entered Henderson's office, a muscle in his right thigh was spasming and jerking so that he could hardly walk. He sat down on a chair across from Henderson's desk. The man stood beside the desk watching him.

"Bynum, you've got a hell of a fighting style." He went into an awkward, off-balance stance, wind milling his arms and kicking one foot at the same time. He burst into laughter, his shoulders shaking and his hands gripping his thighs. Hal began to laugh too, and finally Henderson sat down on the edge of his desk, tears running down his checks. He shook his head, "Oh boy! Oh boy! That's the funniest thing I've ever seen in my life!" He pulled a handkerchief from his hip pocket, wiped the tears from his face and blew his nose loudly.

He looked at Hal for awhile, then said seriously, "Bynum, I'm gonna have to teach you to fight so you don't git killed. I never saw nobody that awkward. You sure you ain't got polio?" He burst into wild laughter again.

And so that was how Hal came to make a pact with violence. It was like living with a mean-assed whore you had to tie up and lock in the bathroom every night so she wouldn't kill you while you were asleep. For thirty years he was to travel with her, smell her foul breath and share her treachery and malice, never knowing when she would turn on him and mete out the same savage retribution he had so often visited on others.

It was a trap that no earthly power could free him from, and many dark years of despair and destruction were to intervene before he could be ready to even entertain the idea that there existed any power greater than an earthly one.

Hal got up, closed the door to the trailer house and went to bed. The rum had eased the pain in his neck enough. He could sleep.

Papa Was a Good Man

It rained all the way to Cincinnati
With our mattress on top of the car
All us kids were eatin' crackers and baloney
Papa kept on drivin', never stopped once at a bar

Then Mama started talkin' about Jesus
And how our lives could be from now on
While Papa bought a used tire in Columbus
Mama rocked the baby till all her tears were gone

She said your Papa is a good man
And don't you kids forget it
The whiskey's tryin' to ruin him
But I know the Lord won't let it
Then we sang Amazing Grace and Bringing In The Sheaves
Rock of Ages, Rock of Ages, cleft for me

I guess we shoulda known Papa never could quit drinkin'
The whiskey had too much of a hold on him
But he loved us, and he did the best he could
And every time our world would start to fall down all around us
Mama would pack everything we owned into some old car, and we'd start for some new town,
And she'd say,

Your Papa is a good man
And don't you kids forget it
The whiskey's tryin' to ruin him
But I know the Lord won't let it
Then we sang Amazing Grace and Bringing in the Sheaves
Rock of Ages, Rock of Ages, cleft for me

Rock of Ages, Rock of Ages, cleft for me

Hal Bynum, Sony Tree/BMI

Rosa's Western Club, 1955

As Hal walked out of the bar a flash of light burst like a Roman candle inside his skull and there was an immediate implosion of pain, which turned to a deadening narcotic almost before it was recorded in his consciousness. For several weeks, or perhaps months, he couldn't tell which, he observed the man who had hit him reset his feet and then begin to throw the left hook at him again. In a detached and almost disinterested manner, Hal wondered why his attacker had not followed with a right and ended the whole thing rather than lose momentum and start at him again with the same punch.

It was as though the camera were stuck and he was seeing each frame frozen and held for an almost interminable length of time as the gravity-grip of unconsciousness beckoned siren-like from the soft sweet darkness of surrender and oblivion. He was outside of time and he knew that somehow this little time-transaction in front of Rosa's Western Club had occurred long before: during the time when he had dwelt in human form on an evolutionary planet, and that the new 1956 Buick behind the man, placed the scene in its own slot in the flowing succession of events.

Suddenly he jerk-snapped back into the film-frame and reentered the motion-movement of violence as he felt his knees began to buckle and lethargy creeping into the network of muscle and sinew that strove valiantly and even heroically to keep him on his feet. There was a sound rolling and spiraling through his head and it quickly became the voice of Bill Henderson hollering at him during a workout.

"When you're hurt, get inside and hold on! Tie him up! Put all your weight on him and ride him around the ring till you've got your strength back."

Hal buried his face in the man's chest, throwing his arms out like grappling hooks in an attempt to capture the arms and smother the punches. He was taller than the bouncer and as he lurched forward, barely making it inside the hook, the top of his head struck the man's mouth and chin and because of the other's forward movement, there was a tremendous impact. The sharp pain of the teeth and jaw-bone cut through the fog and as they fell together, the adrenalin-shock awakening and propelling energy through Hal's body.

On their way to the concrete sidewalk he perceived that the body he had a grip on was suddenly and momentarily lifeless and by a supreme effort Hal was able to twist and haul himself around and land on top of the other body.

With sudden and acute awareness, he saw blood spurting from the mouth and a stunned glaze in the eyes. Hal put all his weight and strength and leverage into a vicious elbow shot. He had aimed at the chin but the head was back and it struck the man's Adam's apple, making an awful whack-thunk sound and Hal saw the man's eyes bulge forward as though they were going to explode from his face. He raised himself to his knees and got all his weight and his returning power into a right hand that landed in the middle of the bloody face.

The floor-bouncer was unconscious; his hands stretched straight out on the sidewalk as though he were nailed to a cross.

Hal stood up and raised his foot high above the bloody and inert face, preparing to stomp the face and throat but a hand reached out and shoved him backward, a loud voice shouting, "Leave him alone, you're gonna kill 'im!"

Hal looked up and saw a crowd moving from the dance floor, past the cash register where the woman took the money and stamped the hands. He glanced around quickly and found his glasses, miraculously unbroken, grabbed them with a quick movement and ran down the dark side of the club and through an alley, his torn shirt making a flapping sound.

The Comeback

You know, I guess every young boy that's ever listened to country music
Has dreamed of singin' on the stage of the Grand Ole Opry
Well I'm one of those who made it - and then lost it
All because of one weakness - whiskey tasted good to me.

I hit the booze hard - then I hit the skids harder
Just fourteen weeks from the Opry to the gutter
But I turned up ten years later - sober
Drivin' a bus for a rock group called "Real Butter"

The lead singer had been takin' funny aspirins
And barkin' like a dog since Denver
When I pulled up behind the Hungry I in Frisco
He broke away from the bass player and dove through a winder

Jingle jangle jingle, country music single
I hear lonesome singin' everywhere I go
Jingle jangle jingle, country music jungle
Ain't you glad we're ridin' in God's big rodeo

Back stage the lead singer was cryin' and bleedin'
An' said if he ever got home to his Mom, he'd never leave her
I eased out to the bus and unlocked my locker
Pulled out my guitar and a pearl gray 3x beaver

I came back in wearin' my D28 Martin and my cowboy hat
And I knew dog gone well it was now or never
I asked the steel man, "Son, can you make a train whistle?"
An' he said, "Right on, Pop, whatever."

I ran out on the stage a smilin'
And the band hit "The Yellow Rose of Texas"
I cocked my cowboy boot out and yodeled
Friends, it hit them kids in the solar plexus.

Jingle jangle jingle, country music single
I hear lonesome singin' everywhere I go
Jingle jangle jingle, country music jungle
Ain't you glad we're ridin' in God's big rodeo

I closed the show with "Amazing Grace"
And got a standing ovation for "The White Cliffs of Dover"
When I came off, them kids were tearin' at my clothes
And I winked at the lead singer and I said,
"You know what pard, I believe I just made me a comeback
This calls for a little celebration.
Didn't I see a fifth of Jack Daniels somewhere backstage?"

Jingle jangle jingle, country music single
I hear lonesome singin' everywhere I go
Jingle jangle jingle, country music jungle
Ain't you glad we're ridin' in God's big rodeo

Hal Bynum, Andite Invasion/BMI From the album It's My Time, 1995

"Kid"

Kid grinned, "Hal tell 'em about some of the shit you used to pull on Bobby Bobo."

Hal took a sip of coffee and smiled, "You'd have to know BoBo. He was a funny sumbitch himself. One of the great thieves of our time. He could get the same guy twice. An artist."

Kid was already laughing and the others were smiling and waiting.

Hal continued, "BoBo's office was in the old 812 building. Where WJRB is now. He really loved humor. This must have been in 1970 or 69. He used to have this secretary. She was a really nice girl, kinda goofy but nice. She's in a rest home out in Madison. She had a stroke a few years ago. I'd start to go in his office and she'd say, 'Hal, you can't go in! Bobby's got his accountant and some people from New York and—' I'd open the door and walk in backwards, making motions with my hands like I was giving direction to somebody. I'd say somethin' like, 'Hold that end higher. Alright, ease it forward! Don't hit it on that desk!' Then I'd turn around to the people settin' around his office and I'd say, 'Would you folks mind standing against that wall for a minute?' They'd all lineup against the wall and then I'd grin at BoBo and leave. He loved it. After I'd leave, he'd tell 'em about what a character I was. A little music city color. Entertainment for the customers."

Hal lit a cigarette, beginning to enjoy himself.

"Anyway, this one time I was pretty drunk and I started into his office and Betty said, 'Hal! You cain't go in! I mean it! Bobby's got Bob Drummond and some investors from New York!' I'd just come from Durwood Hoddock's office, down the hall. He'd been showin' me this double barrel shotgun he'd just had re-blued, and I told Betty, 'Ok baby, I understand,' and walked back to Durwood's office. I asked him if I could go show his shotgun to somebody, I broke it open to make sure it was empty, walked back down the hall, pointed it at Betty and closed the breech. She screamed, which was what I wanted. I reached and opened the door to BoBo's office just a crack, reared back, kicked it open and jumped into the room. I leveled the gun at BoBo and hollered, 'BoBo you've screwed me around long enough!'"

Kid was laughing wildly, scratching the back of his neck like a monkey.

"Everybody took it different, and me and BoBo just watched the commotion. The feller that took it best was an old man with a white mustache. He just froze in his chair and didn't move a muscle. The one who took it the worst was Bob Drummond, the lawyer. There was a little portable record player on the floor next to the wall and he stuck his head into that thing and closed the top down on his neck. He was makin' a whinin', gurglin' sound and his ass was stickin' straight up and shakin'." Hal puffed at the Pall Mall. By now everyone was laughing.

"By that time we were all lookin' at Drummond, kind of amazed at the show he was puttin' on. I reached over, stuck the gun to one cheek of his ass and pulled both triggers. It made a loud snapping sound and Drummond screamed like a panther. You could hear him all the way over to the Tally Ho bar in spite of the noon traffic."

It was fun to tell and relive those stories, but if he did it too often, it all began to look good to him. Pain has no memory and his mind tended to delete the emptiness and loneliness of his drinking years, leaving only the nostalgic lure of the fun times. If he wasn't careful, the stories could become a siren song and pull him toward the rocks and reefs. If there was anything he didn't need, it was alcohol.

"Kid" was Ronnie Sessions. He had begun his career in country music singing and playing his guitar on Cousin Herb Henson's "Town Hall Party" in Los Angeles, when he was nine years old, billed as Oklahoma Ronnie. By the time he was thirteen, he was traveling with package shows and nightclub acts working the West Coast and Las Vegas. He had been drinking and smoking dope ever since. His father was a gambler and bunko artist when Kid was growing up, but by the time Hal knew him, he had done a little time behind the walls and had come out straight. After that he had settled down to his real talent, which was breeding and training racehorses.

Kid was always torn between his mother's gentle goodness and the wild outlaw life he had seen on his dad's side of the family.

Running with the boys he ran with on the streets of Bakersfield and living on the road in honky tonks with a bunch of drunk and pilled up musicians, Kid had had to learn to fight early. He had a real talent for it and a sudden, crazed animal adrenalin frenzy that combined with his fast hands and punching power to produce a vicious efficiency that prevented him having to fight the same person twice. Like Bud Reneau, Kid always tried to avoid fights, but his affability and small stature was an invitation to bullies when they were drinking and wanting to prove a lie.

When Chuck Howard met Kid in Los Angeles. Kid had been on several record labels without any real success and was floating around living off the land. Kid's great gift was that he was totally likeable. He was funny, a natural people pleaser who laughed a lot and had a careful appreciation of other people's personalities. He never had any money. He was the perfect side-kick and somebody in the crowd was always willing to pay his way. However you wanted to be was fine with him. He liked it. As long as there was plenty of excitement.

One evening, Hal was eating in the Flaming Steer restaurant on West End Avenue, near Music Row, when Chuck Howard came in with the handsome blond haired youth beside him and sat down at Hal's table. Chuck was shorter than Kid and through the years when the two would meet and shake hands, Chuck would shout at Kid, "TOO SHORT! YOU'RE TOO SHORT! YOU'LL NEVER MAKE IT AS A SINGER. THEY WANT 'EM TALL LIKE HAWKSHAW HAWKINS! YOU'RE MUCH TOO-SHORT! NEVER MAKE

IT!"

Hal was trying to stay mad over a stolen car Chuck had bought and sold to him, but anyone who had a sense of humor was doomed to love Chuck and forgive him over and over again in an unending rhythm that would have been monotonous had it not been for the excitement Chuck generated everywhere he went, everyday of his life.

As soon as the waitress took their orders and left, Hal jerked his thumb at Kid without turning his gaze from Chuck, "I see you got a new stooge. What happened to the one with the humpback?"

Chuck never went anywhere without a companion to serve as an audience when he was between crowds. Hal always ridiculed the stooge which forced Chuck to calm down whoever it was, explaining Hal to them, undercutting and blunting the attack, smoothing their ruffled feathers so their defensiveness would not become hostility and get in the way of Chuck's show. If the side-kick couldn't take the insults, and finally challenged Hal, Chuck would nod to Hal, wordlessly awarding him the round, and then turn to the stooge and say, "Trust me. This man is very violent and very dangerous and he would like nothing better than for you to jump on him. It would be a disaster for you. Trust me. Hal's extremely insecure. Just go along with me."

Hal saw immediately that there was something different about Ronnie Sessions. One thing was that Chuck made no attempt to protect or shield his feelings. That meant there was no need to. The other thing was that from the first invective Hal dumped on him, no one enjoyed it as much as Kid. He loved it. A light had come on in his eyes and he was obviously savoring the timing, the delivery and the originality and depth of the material. Hal liked him immediately. No one, least of all Hal, could resist that kind of enlightened appreciation.

He didn't find out how funny Kid was until after they were finished eating and Chuck talked Hal into leaving his car in the parking lot and riding with them. Chuck wanted to find Bud Reneau and sell him a Volkswagen they had pieced together, a junkyard at a time, on their trip from L.A. to Nashville.

Chuck had made a right turn on Division Street when Kid suddenly pointed to a laundry and drycleaning establishment on the right.

"Chuck, pull in here an lemme get my cleanin'. I'm outta shirts."

Chuck started to say something, but instead, he turned in and pulled up in front of the shop. It was a drive-in with an open window on one side of the storefront where an old lady sat behind a cash register.

Kid said, "Oh hell. We're too late. That old woman's the only one here and she's already locked up the box that's got the tickets in it and the man that's got the key to it's already gone home and she don't have his number and he took all the money except the silver and you gotta have exact change and the stuff that's on special came in after five o'clock and ain't been sorted. Drive on! I'll get it tomorrow. No, tomorrow's Sunday, I'll have to buy some more clothes. No, the store's closed on Sunday. I'll have to wear my bathrobe. Shit, I wish ta hell Ida brought my bathrobe. It's in the cleaners back home. Drive! Let's go."

As Chuck backed out, Hal exploded with laughter. Chuck didn't laugh. Apparently, he was used to it. As he threaded the car into traffic, he said, "The part about tomorrow being Sunday isn't the funniest part. The funniest part is that he doesn't have any clothes there. The only clothes he's got are the one's he's wearing."

When Hal was finally able to shut off the laughter, he turned and began to carefully study the young man from California. Kid was smiling happily. He hadn't shown Hal his credentials out of any ego need, he had done it to let him know they were on the same level and that Hal could do his best stuff without fear of Kid being puzzled or lost. It was a short-cut. Kid was always in a hurry.

There Ain't No Good Chain Gang

Bet it ain't rainin' back home
Bet ya sister's still on the phone
I bet Mama's in the kitchen
Cookin' fried chicken
Wishin' that I hadn't done wrong

Ah, Mama, don't you worry about it none. Everything's gonna be alright, Mama. When I git back home I might even share some of these things we've learned in here. Things like:

> There ain't no good in an evil hearted woman
> And I ain't cut out to be no Jesse James
> You don't go writin' hot checks down in Mississippi
> And there ain't no good chain gang

Papa's readin' yesterday's mail
Wishin' that the hay was all bailed
I bet Papa is a wishin'
We could go fishin'
But here I am a layin' in jail

Ah Papa don't you worry about me none. We'll be back out on that same ole creek bank, and I might even let you in on some of the things we've learned in here.
  Things like:

> There ain't no good in an evil hearted woman
> And I ain't cut out to be no Jesse James
> You don't go writin' hot checks down in Mississippi
> And there ain't no good chain gang

> There ain't no good in a evil hearted woman
> And I ain't cut out to be no Jesse James
> You don't go writin' hot checks down in Mississippi
> And there ain't no good chain gang

(Hal Bynum and Dave Kirby, Sony/Tree Publishing/BMI From the album, The Promise, 2002)

The Red Quarter, 1975

"What I need is a hit song and a lot of money so I can destroy myself with more style." Hal downed over a third of the beer. "A man ought to be able to have a modicum of dignity while he's makin' a ass out of himself. A little comfort while he's punishin' himself." He took another drink, "I'd like to be ostracized an excluded from better groups."

Hillman was laughing now and his teeth shown white in the darkness of the bar. Hal thought again how much he looked like his brother, Tom T. Hall. It was winter and Hillman was wearing an old denim jumper with a black corduroy collar like the ones that old men who worked in cotton gins wore when Hal was a boy. Hal had one like it at home.

Kid was bored and he called to the waitress, "Darlin' could I have a word with you?"

She was an older woman with dyed black hair and she limped across the room and stood by Kid's chair. On one foot she had a house shoe and on the other a saddle oxford. Kid handed her a check he had just finished writing.

"Hon, could I have five dollars worth of quarters so I can go up front and play the pinball machine?"

She took the check and turned half way around so she could read it by the light of the jukebox. She nodded and limped toward the cash register at the end of the bar.

Hal was about to lose half his audience and didn't like any part of it. He waited till she was almost across the little dance floor and called, "Would you mind holding that check till Wednesday?"

The heavyset woman froze in the middle of a limp and spun her head around. Before Kid could say anything, Hal explained, "It's a good check. There's nothing wrong with it. Just keep runnin' it through. It'll clear."

She came back to Kid, shaking her head and holding the piece of paper at arm's length.

"I'm sorry, but the night manager'll have to O.K. this. She dudn' come in until seven o'clock."

Kid was laughing at the trick. "That's all right dear. I understand."

Hal said, "Bring us another round, I'll pay for it with some cash money I got here."

Hillman had his forehead on the table laughing uncontrollably.

Kid shook his head, still laughing, "You're pretty funny, daddy." It was something Hal's son Christopher had said when he was about three years old and Kid used it a lot.

Hal called to the woman as she was opening the beers. "Bring a red quarter an I'll match you for the jukebox."

Forgiveness

In the early morning clarity he saw it again. It was selfishness and self-centeredness. That was what kept him from forgiving his parents. He had wanted them to be perfect for his sake. He had wanted the woman who had grown up in the little fear-filled farmhouse to suddenly become stable, wise and courageous for his sake. He had wanted the childish and violent alcoholic, wracked with self-loathing and insecurity, to exhibit patience, sagacity and faith in order to be a perfect father to Hal.

In the intervening years he had been just like them and had done worse things than they had done but still he couldn't forgive them. He put the palm of his right hand on the back of his head and worked his neck until it popped and the pain eased. He didn't know where to start. He either had to forgive himself so he could forgive them or he had to forgive them so he could forgive himself. He didn't know where to start.

Christopher

The best relationship Hal had ever had in his life was with his son, Christopher. It was because of the way Christopher was. He had the same kind of deal with nearly everybody. When the little boy came around, people's faces lit up and they stopped whatever they were doing to pass some time with him. He didn't confront or approach people, he went about his little business and when they called to him, he would stop and talk. He was a little bit shy but, he liked everybody and that made people feel good about themselves. Hal took him to the A. A. Clubhouse with him and while his dad was in meetings, Christopher liked to visit with whoever was working at the snack bar. When he got to know them, he would joke with them and then they would tell other people what he had said and everybody would pass it around and laugh about it.

A neighbor told Christopher's mother that he had learned more from Christopher than anybody. Cynthia asked, "Like what?"

The man told her a story. He said that when Christopher had gotten his new bike, a lady across the street had been admiring it and Christopher told her he was going to put reflectors on the spokes of his bike, as soon as he found some clothes pins. The woman went into her house and came back with however many clothespins he needed. A few days later, the man who was telling the story saw Christopher messing with his bike and asked him what was wrong. Christopher had a piece of wire and was trying to use it instead of a clothespin he had lost. The man suggested he go ask the same lady for another clothespin. Christopher looked sad and shook his head.

"I'd be embarrassed for her to know I lost it." He picked up the wire again, studying the problem.

The man thought a few seconds and then said, "Tell her it broke."

Christopher looked at the man with surprise. "I can't do that. I don't tell lies."

The neighbor told Cynthia that there was nothing judgmental about the way he said it, he was just explaining why the idea wouldn't work. He laughed and mentioned how the scriptures said something about 'A little child will lead them.'

It was the same with Hal only more so. Knowing the little boy since he was a baby and watching him grow was the most valuable experience in Hal's life. It had made a profound change in him. Hal had once read a definition of wisdom that he agreed with. It said that wisdom was love and intelligence. Christopher was the most deeply intelligent person Hal had ever met and he was entirely motivated by love and kindness, and that was where the wisdom came from.

His judgment was always better than Hal's; which wasn't a particularly high recommendation, but the truth was that he was wiser than anyone Hal had known intimately. Part of it was that Christopher didn't twist the truth in order to feel better about himself. He felt good about himself the way he was. He neither wanted nor needed to deal in superlatives.

Once after an ice-hockey game, Hal was squatting in front of Christopher as he sat on a bench and changed his clothes. His hair was pressed down from wearing the helmet and his face was red from the cold.

Hal said, "Christopher, you're the best player on the team!"

The boy who played goalie had been sick and Christopher had let the other team score only once. He was pulling a skate off and when Hal paid him the compliment, he stopped and looked up at his dad.

"No. I'm not the best. I'm the third best." He named the two boys whom he considered to be better than him.

He never wanted to mix any unreality in with reality. He didn't care to turn the kaleidoscope.

One of his talents was as a peacemaker. Virginia, Hal's third wife, had been the first one to notice it. She explained it to Hal and then he began to see it himself. When a disagreement between adults threatened to become heated, Christopher, even at that age, would find a way to intervene. He would ask a question, make a request, or in some other way attempt to divert the conversation long enough to diffuse the building anger.

When Christopher was about nine years old, Hal decided to tell him he knew about his efforts as a harmonizer in order to encourage him and praise him for it. The boy listened without making any comment. Hal ended by saying, "And I know why you do it"

"Why?"

"Because you can't stand to see anybody's feelings get hurt."

Christopher quickly nodded in agreement, "Yeah, like for instance, mine!"

Christopher had found out soon after his parents' marriage broke up, that when Cynthia and Hal were having trouble it was easy for him to get caught in the middle. For the first few years Hal was still boozing and smoking dope or else he was irritable and crazy from withdrawal, whereas Cynthia was still afraid of him and sour because their divorce came before he made it big in the business. They were both nervous people, and sometimes when Hal would accidentally find out that Cynthia had spanked Christopher or slapped him in the face, it would be all he could do to keep from going over to her house, pulling her out in the yard and beating her half to death. This was the cauldron in which Christopher's skills as a tranquilizer and a politician were forged.

A year or so after Hal bought the house a block from Cynthia's house, Kid and Hal were sitting around the den smoking a little dope and Kid mentioned that he hadn't seen Christopher in months. They drove over and parked in her driveway. When they got out, there were some kids standing in front of the garage and Hal asked them where Christopher was. A boy pointed to a window above the garage.

"He can't get out."

They looked up and saw the little boy sitting quietly, watching them through the window of the rock house. He looked sad and forlorn, but calm.

"What do you mean, he can't get out?"

"The baby sitter locked him in and took Jennifer somewhere."

Hal remembered that none of the rooms could be opened from the inside without a key. He motioned for Christopher to meet him at the top of the basement steps.

Kid said, "What'd be nice would be if that damn house caught on fire. There wouldn't be no way in the world for him to get out!"

"That's what I was thinking."

They stood on the top step and talked through the door.

"Christopher, where's the key?!"

"Sondra took it with her."

"Where'd they go?"

"I don't know."

"Where's your mother?"

"She's working."

"Do you know what studio?"

"No."

"Christopher, I want you to open a window on the first floor and come outside. I don't want you locked in there." He didn't mention fire.

"I can't, they're all nailed. Mom and Robert nailed them shut because of the antiques."

While they had been talking, Kid had been working on the lock with a knife. "The only way you can get in this door is with an axe."

"It'd serve her right if I chopped the son of a bitch into kindlin' wood," Hal whispered. The rage he had been feeling toward the babysitter was rapidly spreading to include Cynthia.

Christopher's voice came through the door, calm and helpful, "I can get out of my window." Then after a few moments, "But there's nothing to climb down on."

Kid ran down the stairs and searched the garage. He came back.

"No ladder. You got a ladder at your house?"

"No." Hal took out the pipe and they had a few hits of marijuana.

"Dad, there's another window. It's got a roof outside it."

"Go see if you can open it."

"Okay." They heard his footsteps receding. In a little while he was back.

"Dad, I got it open."

"Does it have a screen on it?"

"No."

"Christopher, you go look out of the window. We're gonna come around there." They walked around the back of the house and along the side until they saw him leaning out of the window over a small peaked side roof.

There was a gutter at the bottom. It was about twelve feet to the ground.

Hal and Kid discussed it and reached up as high as they could. They decided they could catch him, "Christopher, I want you to climb out on the roof and then start sliding your butt and your feet real slow till you get down to this gutter. Then you can drop down and Kid and me'll catch you."

Christopher studied the roof and then looked down at them. It was a long way. "Dad, I'm scared."

"It'll be alright, pretty boy. We'll catch you. It'll work."

"Dad, I don't want to."

"Christopher, it's the right thing to do. Have I ever told you anything that wadn't right?"

"No."

He climbed through the window and began to slowly make his way down the gritty roofing. When he got to the bottom, he half turned and took hold of the gutter.

Kid whispered, "I hope that damned gutter don't tear loose."

Christopher lowered himself until his arms were straight and he was hanging full length. His feet were about a yard above their reach.

"Let go, Christopher, we've got you."

His hands released the gutter and they grabbed him. Before his feet had quite touched the ground he said, "Boy! Am I glad that's over!" Then his feet were on the ground and without a break in his movement, he trotted around in a little circle, shaking his head and blowing out his breath. Kid and Hal burst into laughter, and Hal picked Christopher up and kissed him on his face and head.

They all laughed and talked and Kid did a take-off on the way Christopher had started expressing his relief, before he was completely on the ground. But driving to his house, a picture of the little boy trapped and terrorized by fire came back to Hal and the rage took him again.

Christopher was always alert to his moods and thoughts and he watched Hal's face in the light from the dashboard. "Dad?"

"Yeah."

"Somebody's got to tell Mom about this. Who do you think ought to tell her?" Before Hal could answer he said quickly but casually, "I was just thinking that I might tell her. Would that be alright?"

Hal sighed, "I guess so. That might be the best way to handle it." He got a quick picture of what the scene could be like. A raging confrontation, leading to who knew what.

"So that's the way we'll do it? You don't say anything to her? I'll tell her about it?"

"Okay, pretty boy, that'll be alright."

Kid passed him the pipe and he took a puff on it as they got out of the car behind Hal's house. Christopher ran into the house to turn on the T.V. set as the two men stood behind the car and smoked.

Kid laughed, "Boy he's a hell of a politician. Probably the smoothest I've ever seen. He knew if you got into it with Cynthia, it'd be a hell of a deal and one way or another he'd wind up in the middle. He didn't want no part of that."

"Yeah." Hal was looking at the yellow moon above the dark trees. When he had bought the house, he had been going to the alcoholic rehabilitation meetings long enough to know that he couldn't control what went on in the other house. He couldn't control anyone but himself and most of the time, he couldn't even do that. He had spent a hundred and seventy grand to be near his son to build him up and make him feel more secure and he knew he couldn't do it by quarreling with Cynthia.

When he had moved in he had told her, "I haven't moved over here to cause you trouble. I've moved here to try to help in anyway I can. I don't want to try to run anything, I just want to take as much load off of you as I can, baby-sitting, haulin' him places, whatever. I don't want to get in your way, I want to be a help."

After a while, she began to see that he meant what he said and they had begun to work together, more or less amicably. They both had good intentions, but it was the child's wisdom and love that lead them and made it work.

Last Summer

There was a kitty in the window
and a picture of a pony on the wall
I held his hand and read him stories
as summer turned to fall

He'd missed alot of school that year, and by the time summer came, he was spendin' most of his days in bed. I'd prop him up with pillows, and we'd look out the window at the squirrels and the birds, and the way the trees and the bushes and the flowers changed with the season, and the way the back yard looked different at different times of the day. He had a calico cat that had loved him all his life, and she sat on the windowsill and watched him from daylight 'til dark. She knew somethin' was wrong.

Lookin' back, it was the most beautiful time of my life. He'd always been interested in everything and curious about everything, and he always wanted me to tell him stories about when I was a boy his age. Later in the summer, he began to ask me questions about God, and about Heaven, and one day when the leaves were turnin' color, he was quiet for a long time, and then he asked me,
　"Dad, does everything die?"
We were sittin' side by side, lookin' out the window, and when I got to where I could talk, I said,
　"No, son. Life is about love, and love never dies, and anything that's about love never dies. The soul is all about love and so, of course, it never dies. People live forever, if they want to."
He turned his face toward me and squeezed my hand and he said,
　"I want to."
After awhile I said,
　"Son, life is a journey that goes on forever, and we keep on learnin' from the ones ahead of us an teachin' it to the ones behind us an we just keep growin' an sharin' an learnin' to love. This little part of it here is just the first little bit. It gets better an better the further we go."

We both had a project that summer. Mine was to experience and absorb and memorize his goodness, and to try to get him ready for the trip he was gonna be takin' pretty soon. His project was to learn to play "Good Night Irene" on the guitar while I sang it. When he was little I'd sing it to him, 'cause I didn't know any children's bedtime songs, an sometimes I'd think he'd gone to sleep while he was sayin' his prayers, an I'd start to tip-toe out of the room an he'd open his eyes an say "Night, Night Irene!" An I'd come back an do it, and before I finished, he'd be sound asleep.

That summer, I showed him where to put his fingers on the guitar, an he'd practice 'til he couldn't hold his hands up anymore. He'd always been a hard tryer.

In September the storms came an the squirrels and birds went wherever they go when it's rainin', an there was nothin' to see outside, an he spent more an more time practicin' that song. Me singin' it slow, waitin' for him to catch up, him strugglin' to get it right.

Now, sometimes at night, when I wake up an can't get back to sleep, I'll go in his empty room an pull a chair over by the side of his bed, an just sit there with the moonlight comin' in the window, and think about that last summer.

Irene, goodnight
Irene, goodnight
Goodnight Irene
Goodnight Irene
I'll see you in my dreams.

I'll see you in my dreams.

(Hal Bynum, Andite Invasion/BMI From the album If I Could Do Anything 1998 "Goodnight Irene" used by permission from TRO-LUDLOW Music Inc.)

"Lucille"

When Hal pulled into his driveway in Green Hills, his girlfriend, Yvonne, was coming out. She backed up, turned around and they both parked and went into the house. Every time he saw her new yellow Lincoln, it made him feel more dissatisfied with his old gray '80 model Coupe De Ville. He had bought a new Cadillac every year since 1977 and this time his business manager, Ralph Gordon, had said "no." Hal had more sense than to hire somebody to tell him what to do and then not to do it, but the gray car looked awful when it was dirty and Hal could never remember to get it washed.

He reheated the morning coffee and poured them both a cup. He sat down on the couch and she sat on the love seat. Hal pulled off his boots and his shirt, unbuckled his pants and lay back.

Yvonne studied him. "Are you tired?"

"Yeah. No, not really. I was jist thinkin' about something that bothers me when I think about it. One of them deals."

"Oh boy. I'm afraid to ask."

"No, nothin' like that. That woman that's doin' a magazine article wuz talkin' about Kenny an I got to thinkin' about that award show in L.A. when I was blind drunk an embarrassed Kenny an Butler an everybody."

"Oh, the thing where you 'showed your ass' in front of sixty five million people? I heard you mention it in a meeting one time."

"Sixty million. Yeah, that one. I never did tell you about it?" He tried to sip the coffee but it was still too hot.

"No, you didn't. I think Kid or someone mentioned it once and ya'll laughed about it."

"Well anyway, what happened was —well Virginia and me had made a deal where I'd try to control my drinking durin' the trip, but of course I didn't. It had gone bad the first night we were in L.A. A girl from BMI had got tickets to the Palomino. George Jones was working the Palomino an by the time we got out there, I was drunk as a monkey. We went back stage an believe it or not George was sober. Before he realized how damn drunk I was, he asked me if I'd come up and sing "Lucille." Virginia was shakin' her head and signalin' but it didn't work. I told 'im I would. When I got up there I insisted on playin' his guitar an he stood beside me an gripped the back of my shirt with his right hand to hold me up. It was awful. The only good thing about it was hearin' George sing harmony with me on the bridge.

"When the show was over, I wanted to stay and pitch songs to George. There were tons of people around him backstage. He was trying to visit with them and do some business with the club owner and talk to some jocks, and there I was, fallin' down drunk and strummin' his guitar and singin' a bunch of songs to him. The girl from BMI had to get home to go to work the next day and Virginia couldn't get me to leave so she put a twenty in my pocket and told me to take a cab back to the hotel."

Hal lit a cigarette and sipped the coffee, looking past Yvonne into the back yard. Around the periphery of the time corridor were the images of all the times he had pulled the same drunken stunt on most of the other big country singers who were, or had been, his friends. Glen Campbell had been one of the most patient and understanding, but after Hal had inflicted him with three or four episodes, Glen had become disgusted and avoided him from then on.

"At one point, I went back out in the club to look for Virginia, cause by then I'd forgot her leavin' and forgot the twenty in my suit coat pocket, an I ran in to Gilley an his manager, Sherwood Cryer. Sherwood introduced me to Gilley an tol' me they wanted to hear some of my songs. Then the next memory I've got was standin' in the parkin' lot, cussin' out Norro Wilson, who's a good friend of mine an has always treated me great. The next was of me getting out of the cab in front of the hotel an goin' up to the desk an someway gettin' money to pay the cab driver. Then I was on the wrong floor looking for our room, an then I was jerkin' Virginia out of bed an slappin' an hittin' her for leavin' me way the hell across town with no money, as she was screamin' an cryin' an tellin' me to look in my pocket." Hal stopped and took a big drag of smoke and then let it out in a long sigh. His hands were shaking with emotion.

"I felt in the right coat pocket an found the twenty dollar bill."

They both sat and looked at each other for awhile an then he said, "You don't want to hear all this." What he meant was, that he didn't want to tell it.

"Yes, I do. It's like all those stories I heard about you before I saw you drunk. I couldn't believe them. I can now. I can just see it."

"Well, anyway — it was a couple of days till the awards an I would drink till about one or two in the afternoon an then eat a big lunch an take a long nap. That worked pretty good an we figured I could manage to be alright for the presentation. But, like all the jury rigged, half-assed plans of alcoholics, it fell apart.

"The mornin' of the awards, I ran into Billy Parker from KVOO in Tulsa. He was getting the D.J. award that year and we started drinkin' whiskey in the lounge an tellin' sea stories an when it came time to eat an take a nap, I wouldn't eat. We kept drinkin' whiskey and I wouldn't listen to Virginia or Chuck Howard, who was stayin' in the same hotel. I was wearin' a white tuxedo like I had when we got the CMA award an when we went in I had a great big drink of whiskey in my hand. The program started, an while the other awards were bein' given out, I passed out in my seat."

"Oh. No!"

"Oh, yes. All of a sudden they started playing "Lucille" and I jumped up. Virginia tried to get me to sit down, cause it wasn't my award, it was Butler's for bein' the producer. Ray Price and his wife, Janie, were sittin' in front of us. He turned around an took holt of my sleeve an tried to explain it to me, but I didn't believe 'im an went up on the stage. After Butler got the award and said whatever he said, I stepped up and made the acceptance speech I had written on the plane. It was a mess. Nobody knew what to do or say, an some girls came out an led us off stage. When we got backstage, the woman who was runnin' the deal got me by the arm an told me that I had to go back out front an sit down cause I still had to get my award later in the show. Somebody took me around to the lobby an I went down front an set down again. About the time I dozed off to sleep again, they started playin' "Lucille" and I jumped up again. Virginia, an Price an this time Janie, all tried to stop me but I ran up on the stage again. I didn't remember bein' up there before. This time it was Kenny gettin' his award for album of the year an when he got through talkin', I stepped up an made that idiotic speech again. By this time the audience (everybody in Nashville was seated on the right side of the auditorium) knew what was goin' on, an they loved it. They gave me a standin' ovation when I said that deal again."

Yvonne had covered her eyes with embarrassment. "Oh, my God!"

"Yeah. So then, goin' off the stage, I still didn't know there was anything wrong. I said somethin' to Kenny an he just turned his head the other way. That same lady was there an she got me aside an explained it to me again an told me I had to go back an set down cause my award was next. Only this time she didn't send nobody with me and I got lost. I wound up in the balcony an couldn't find my way out. About that time they started playin' the song again. I ran down to the front of the balcony, grabbed the iron railing, hung myself over and dropped into the aisle below. Some woman screamed and there was a commotion, but I got up an ran down the aisle an on the stage and got the award. I was breathin' hard, an you couldn't understand anything I said."

Hal leaned forward and lit a cigarette. "The guy who should have got an award was whoever edited that show. He used close-ups, to get me out of the scenes I wasn't supposed to be in an clipped out the speeches I wasn't supposed to make. He took the best one an replaced the one where I was puffin' and blowin'. You couldn't tell I'd even had a drink when they aired it a couple of weeks later."

Yvonne shook her head. "Kenny must hate you. That's sad isn't it?"

"Well, I don't guess he does. He's a good cat. He's sure of who he is, when somebody else makes an ass out of themselves, he don't see his own reflection in them."

Yvonne said tiredly, "I know, it's all done with mirrors."

"Right."

Song of the Overseas Birds

During my sickness
They flew me to Europe
and kept me in a
sun-blanched room.
Once a day, a doctor and a priest
would visit me, and they would
sit silently on opposite sides of
the bed until at last the
priest would open a leather
bag and remove a large
tablecloth which he would
unfold, and using
two wooden sticks
he had also brought in the
black bag, stuff the tablecloth up my rear end, all except
one corner.

The priest and the doctor
would sit back down
in their chairs and begin to chant
softly with their eyes closed.
Outside I could hear the
sound of birds chirping and singing.
Perhaps because of my discomfort
it seemed like a long ceremony.
At last the priest would
cross himself and then stand
up straight and take a deep
breath before he bent down,
and took hold of the protruding
corner of the tablecloth and
ripped it out, shouting, "Hah!"

The doctor would take the
cloth by the same corner,
between his thumb
and his forefinger and carry
it to a large pan of kerosene
and drop it in.

He would then take the sticks
and swish the cloth back
and forth and then drop the
sticks into the pan.
I could hear their heavy
breathing and the sound of the birds.

After a time I was back in
Cincinnati and
as I began to get well,
everyone told me I had
been delirious and had never
left Ohio.
But I don't believe it.
I can still hear the
unintelligible song
of the overseas birds.

Fair Park Auditorium, 1956

The first time he met Jim Reeves was at the Fair Park auditorium in Lubbock. Hal was backstage with a tape recorder, waiting for a chance to play songs to whoever would listen.

It was a KDAV show, and Dave Stone and Highpockets Duncan always let Hal, Buddy Holly, and Sunny Curtis and the others who played and sang on the Sunday afternoon "live music" program come back and visit and mingle with the big names from Nashville or Shreveport.

Johnny Cash was traveling in an old beat up blue Dodge with Luther and Marshall. Cash was nervous, ill at ease and in awe of the other performers. After he and the Tennessee Two had their instruments more or less in tune, he spent most of his time back stage posing with Ferlin Husky, Jim Reeves and Minnie Pearl, while Luther, the stone-faced guitar player snapped innumerable pictures.

At the time, Hal's hero was Ferlin Husky. As a performer, Ferlin had a magnetism and a presence that moved him more than anyone since as a boy he had been awed and enthralled by the tremendous power and electricity of Al Jolson.

On stage, Ferlin was a devastating comedian. Back stage, he was serious. It would take Hal years to find out that the people who were funny on stage and the people who were funny off stage were almost never the same people.

Looking back, Hal realized that the quality that made Ferlin such an attractive and engaging personality was his honesty. When Cash asked Ferlin to let Luther take their picture, Ferlin stood on tip-toe, his arm around the taller man's shoulder. After the camera snapped and they relaxed the pose, Ferlin giggled, "I don't know why I always have to look taller in pictures than I really am, but I do. Somethin' about it bothers me, I guess."

Later Hal would come to believe that humility was nothin' more or less than self-honesty, but this night, as a naked 100 watt bulb glared down on the little people in the shabby dressing room, he didn't know any of these things.

He had set Homer's tape recorder against the wall, out of the way, and he asked Ferlin to hear the first cut, a novelty song call "Coonshine."

Hal, Buddy Holly, and Ferlin squatted around the machine, looking at the reels as they turned, listening to Homer's voice and Sam Hodge's Merle Travis styled guitar accompaniment as the other performers and musicians moved around them, carrying their instruments and stage clothes.

Buddy seemed unimpressed, although he would mention the song to Hal several years later, shortly before he was killed. Buddy had a record out on Decca at the time, "Blue Days and Black Nights," and he was acting cocky and very knowledgeable about the music business that night. Buddy

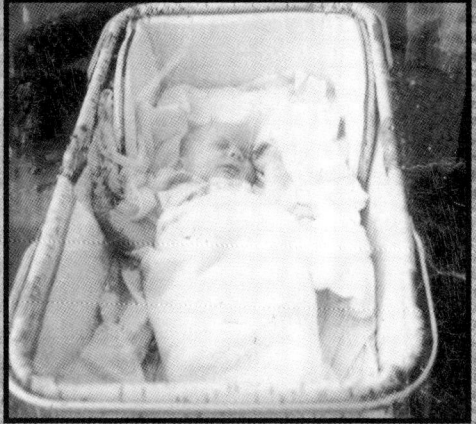

Hal's childhood

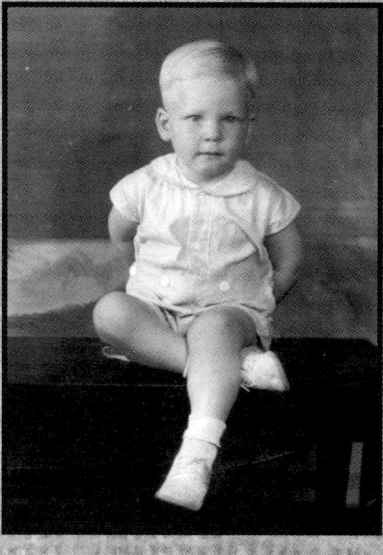

Hal's childhood

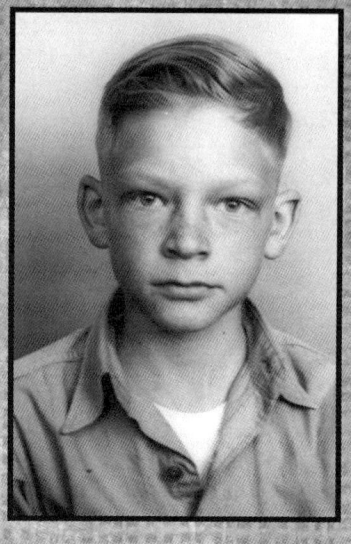

Hal with his parents
in the 1940's.

Hal's grandparents, Tom and Lee Bynum

Hal's parents, Tom & Maggie Bynum
in the 1940's.

Performing "Lucille" at the Truckers Convention in St. Louis. Pam Raymond & Hillman Hall sing backup.

Hal and Johnny Cash after Cash recorded "Papa Was a Good Man" in 1971.

Christopher Bynum

Music City News, 1978

Hal and Dave Kirby performing
"There Ain't No Good Chain Gang" in 1978

Bennie Martin

Chuck Howard, Sr.
circa 1975

Ronnie Sessions "Kid"

"Bud" Reneau, Billy Don Burns and Dobie Gray at Hal & Rebbeca's Wedding, June 12, 1993

Hal's sister, Mary Jo Colegrove; and niece, Deborah Pecorelli, 1993

Hal and Rebecca, June 12, 1993

was a good boy and Hal liked him. He had so much more talent than Hal, that normally Hal would have resented him, but from the first night he had seen Buddy work between acts at the Cotton Club, he had felt the identification with him that people always feel when they are one of the early discoverers of a legend.

Ferlin liked "Coonshine" and thought it would be a good record for Bill Carlisle. Buddy stood up and began talking to someone while "Pay Her a Compliment" was playing, but Ferlin listened to the song without comment. When it finished and Hal turned the machine off, Ferlin mentioned "Coonshine" again and Hal asked him if he would record it himself. Ferlin looked a little uncomfortable and arose, brushing the wrinkles from his pants.

"Well, I've just cut a bunch of things as Simon Crum, I don't know how all that's gonna work out anyway."

A boy about twelve years old plucked at Ferlin's arm and asked if he could sell pictures for him. Ferlin took a stack of black and white eight by ten glossies out of his guitar case and handed them to the boy, telling him he should get fifty cents a piece for them. The boy hurried out of the dressing room, clutching the pictures. He never came back with the pictures or the money.

Johnny Cash was squatting on the floor, strumming and singing a song to Jim Reeves. When he finished. Reeves looked up at Ferlin and laughed, "When this boy gets his growth, he's gonna have a deep voice."

Hal noticed the red light on the recorder and turned the machine off. He sat down in a folding chair against the wall and watched the three performers as they chatted and laughed. He felt empty and defeated.

There was a fiddle player standing close by, and Reeves took the instrument and rosined the bow. He started playing an old fiddle tune and Ferlin got out his guitar and began to accompany him.

When Ferlin would miss a chord change, Reeves would call it out, only slightly condescending, standing erect and majestic, oblivious of the squeaking and squawking sound coming from the fiddle. He was completely at ease, enjoying himself.

When they finished. Reeves returned the fiddle and walked toward the auditorium, where Johnny Cash was singing "Cry, Cry, Cry."

As Ferlin was putting his guitar back in its case, Hal sidled up to him and told him how much he had liked "Gone," which Ferlin had recorded as Terry Preston several years before.

Ferlin looked up at him with real interest. "You know that record was about to hit when Hank Williams died. When that happened, the jocks pulled everything off the air but him. I've been thinkin' about cuttin' it again with a pop arrangement, maybe under a different name so if the jocks don't like it, it won't mess up what I'm doin'."

Hal was excited by talking business with a recording artist. "I think it would hit! I loved the Terry Preston record. It has a weird background!"

"Yeah, Cliffie Stone was playing bass fiddle with a bow, there was an accordion and a steel-" He shook his head and stood up. He sighed, "Who knows, it might be worth a try."

"Where'd you come up with the name Ferlin Husky? That's a funny name!" Hal didn't want the conversation to end.

"That's my real name." He took the coat to his white western styled suit from a hanger and put it on. His mind was somewhere else.

Hal got up and walked toward the door that led to the auditorium, feeling left out again.

Jim Reeves was standing outside the door, studying Cash's performance. The building was full of people, and they were electrified by the gaunt young man's performance. When he finished "Folsom Prison Blues," the crowd exploded.

Hal put his mouth close to Reeves' ear. "I've got some songs on tape and I'd like for you to hear them."

Reeves was wearing charcoal slacks and a sport coat. He was handsome, straight-backed and serious, he pulled his eyes from the stage and said, "I heard the songs."

Anger hit Hal and the blood pounded in his head. "You didn't hear them! But I don't care. You don't have to hear them."

Reeves head jerked toward him, his face flushing, his mouth opening to say something, but then he relaxed and studied the tall, skinny youth for a few seconds. Something softened in his face and he said, "Alright, I heard them, but I'll come back and listen to the tape again. I want to watch the rest of his act."

Hal walked back into the dressing room and sat down to wait.

Minnie Pearl and Ferlin were standing talking about her husband who was a pilot. Apparently he flew Minnie and some of the other Grand Ole Opry members from one date to another in a chartered plane.

Hal heard the crowd screaming and applauding. The roar kept on until Cash started singing "Folsom Prison Blues" again.

Reeves came back in and nodded to Hal. They both squatted down by the recorder and Hal turned it on. He let it warm up and then they listened to "Coonshine" and "Pay Her a Compliment." He had thought Reeves might be interested in the latter song, as it had the same mood as "Yonder Comes a Sucker" which was a big record for him at the time, but when it finished he said,

"You ought to get "Coonshine" to Bill Carlisle. He's looking for something like that. Old Bill could sell you a lot of records. He could have another "No Help Wanted" or "Too Old to Cut the Mustard" anytime. Even if it weren't that big a seller you'd make a lot of air play off it."

Hal started to say that he wasn't interested in a Bill Carlisle record but Reeves said, "I'm not particularly looking for a novelty song. I want to hit with a ballad." He reached behind him and took his guitar out of its case.

"Let me show you the kind of thing I'm looking for." He took a pick from his coat pocket, strummed a chord, re-tuned one string, strummed it again and then said, "I was in Wichita Falls last night and a fellow sang me this song. I had him sing it to me again and then I sang it back to him. See what you think of it." He began to sing "My Lips Are Sealed," and all of Hal's frustration and hostility melted as the beautiful baritone voice, smooth, warm and intimately vibrant, rose and fell and gently led Hal through the story of the song.

The style was different than anything Reeves had done before and it had a tremendous impact on Hal. For some reason, he thought of Nat "King" Cole. Before he could tell Jim how powerfully it affected him, Johnny Cash called to Reeves from the other side of the room where he had Luther standing by to take more pictures.

Buddy was talking with the Nashville people and the little 'in' group of radio station fans who always managed to get backstage. Jerry Allison, the boy who was his drummer, was clowning, laughing and strutting through the evening. He was frenetic, flaky and a pain-in-the-ass, from Hal's viewpoint.

Years later, Hal would look back at the drummer, Cash and himself and see three young men with a tendency toward personality isolation, driven by the fear of personality isolation toward center stage and the spotlight, that place which is the place of greatest personality isolation.

But that night as Hal carried the tape recorder and hitch-hiked back to the college campus, all he could see was that it was going to be a much harder struggle than he had imagined. Of the three recording artists, he felt that Ferlin was the only one who would help him, and in those days whoever would help him was his hero.

All three of them would almost immediately emerge as superstars, and although Ferlin's and Hal's careers would never cross paths, Jim Reeves and Johnny Cash would become not only warm friends, but major stepping stones in his own success story.

You could never tell how it would all turn out, which was good.

An Old Man's Prayer

An old man slowly sat himself down in a lawn chair under a giant oak tree on a summer afternoon, lettin' the long sigh go out through his lips as a whistle, then wiggled and grunted himself around till he was comfortable.

After a short spell he began to talk quietly, as if to another person, "Lord, it gits harder fer me to git up an git down ever day. I'm about wore out an it seems like my sight's about to go out on me. Acourse what little I do, don't take a whole lot of seein' to git it done.

"Instead of bein a help, I'm mostly in the way an everbody gits wore out hollerin' at me, tryin' to git me to hear what they're sayin'.

"I try not to stand in the way, though. I remember sayin' to Estel one time, back when we was both young and strong, 'Estel, why do old people always git right whur people need to go an jist stand there? Looks like they'd see that you're tryin' to git around 'em an move!'

"I know you remember it, Lord. You remember everthaing an know everthaing ebm before it happens. Let's see, what was I gonna say?

"Oh, Estel said, 'Jarad, someday you an me will get old an we'll be just like they are. Unless sumpin' happens to us before then.

An we'll stand right in the way an won't know what to do anymore an the kids'll call you Papaw an it'll all come around to us before you know it.'

"Estel was quite a woman. She knew a goodeal. She was a wise person an Lord, how she loved you. She didn't preach to people an she didn't talk about you much out in public, jist when we was by ourself. She talked allot about how much she loved you and how grateful she was that she'd known you all her life. An later, she'd say little prayers with the children an —.

"Lord amercy what in the world?! Oh, that's them people that bought the old Peterson place. That woman comes through here like a Zeplin in that rig she drives. They call it by some letters. Let's see, SUB no, SUV. She's got no more use for that thaing than the man in the moon.

"Lemeeseenow, Lord, I was talkin' to you about....oh, Estel. You're the only one that'll ever know how much I miss her. She was my whole life. I'll never - Oh well, you know all that. She's with you now an I'm glad about that, but — oh, oh, no — nobody knows.

"Here I am boy! Out here under this tree. Comon! Comon Beau. You're gittin' blinder'n me. Ataboy. Jist lay right down here by my feet. You cain't jump up in my lap nomore. That's alright. You're my boy. Yeah, you still like to gittchi ears rubbed. I don' know what I'd do without you, little man.

"Lord, sometimes I'm tempted to ask you to take me before this little dog goes. I don't know if I can stand to bury another piece of my heart. But I'd hate to thaink how he'd be after I was gone. I didn't thaink he was gonna make it after Estel left us.

It musta been close to a month he lay outside her bedroom door, his little nose restin' on the carpet. He'd look up at me outta the top of his little brown eyes. He finally got up an around, but ever once in awhile he'll wake up from a nap an go scratch on her door. He forgets she's gone.

"Everythaing an everbody has to move on an keep on livin' whatever happens. I've always trusted you, Lord, an that's got me through everthaing an kep me reasonably happy. I know these years without my girl are a test, an it's brought me closer to you. She used to tell me that if we'll let whatever pain an suffering that comes our way - push us closer to you, then it's all worth it.

"Pretty soon we'll start gittin' some cool mornin's an the first thaing you know, it'll be wintertime. Time gits on by.

"This'll be me an Beau's first Christmas without Estel. You'll have to help me Lord. But then .... you always do."

Hal Bynum, Andite Invasion/BMI From the album, The Promise, 2002

The World's Greatest Fiddle Player

Benny Martin was a character. He should have been in movies. He was almost as wide as he was tall, and his appearance, his powerful personality, and his talent made a tremendous impact on people. He was one of the greatest showmen, on or off the stage, that Hal had ever seen.

Benny and Hal had loved one another from the moment they met. They both enjoyed a good, fast rolling show. They had both lived lives of violence, and no matter how gentle they were now, the old wild, cornered animal craziness still seeped through and provided people with a tingle of excitement they didn't quite understand.

Hal had been a fan of Benny's since he had heard him play on Johnnie and Jack's records in the early fifties, and on Benny's own hit record, "Ice Cold Love," but they didn't get acquainted until 1975 when someone introduced them at an alcoholic rehabilitation meeting. Bennie had been Hank Williams' closest friend, but he didn't tell Hal until the summer of 1981, when Benny talked him into working the road with him, that Hal had always reminded him of Hank.

"I hadn't told you about it, Brother, cause I didn't want to depress you, on account of you being a alcoholic and Hank bein' a alcoholic that died from it, but the first night I wuz around you, it put goose bumps on my arm how much you reminded me of Hank." Benny was leaning over a plate of fish, squinting at Hal because of an allergy that made his eyes burn. He had Abraham Lincoln chin whiskers with no mustache. "It ain't jist because you're tall and bald headed like he wuz, it's the way you write and talk and move. Ebm the way you hunker down over the mike when you sing."

Hal was shocked, finding it hard to believe. "Are you shitting me?"

Bennie turned to his wife. "Thelma, tell him what I told you the night I introduced you to Hal."

Thelma was a tall handsome woman who looked part Indian. She spoke in rapid, machine gun bursts, "When me and Benny got back in the camper, I started to turn the keys on and he reached across an put his hand on my arm and stopped me. He said, 'Thelma, you asked me one time what Hank Williams was like and I couldn't explain it to you. That man right there is so much like him it scares me. Everything he does is like him!'"

Benny picked up a hush puppy, started to pop it in his mouth but dropped it back in his plate, shaking his head sadly. He was trying to lose weight.

"That's right. That's right. That's what I told 'er." Benny looked through the window at the cars in the parking lot. "When Hank came in a place, everybody watched him. They listened to everything he said. They wanted to be around 'im." He looked back at Hal. "It's the same way with you. When you come on stage at the fiddlers convention and started singin', I turned around to my brother, Gene, on rhythm guitar, and I said in his ear,

'Gene, who does he remind you of? And Gene said, 'Hank.'"

Hal knew Benny was telling him the truth, but it didn't make sense to him. He had never seen Hank in person or on film, if there were any such films.

Bennie took the napkin out of the neck of his shirt, dropped it on the top of his plate and leaned back in his chair, "Your melodies aren't like Hank's but they've got the same lonesome sound and they stick in people's minds the way his did."

Yvonne was watching Hal, a look of speculation on her face. "Does this mean you have to drink yourself to death?"

They all laughed and Hal said, "You're pretty funny, Pretty."

Bennie was from east Tennessee and his people were mountain people. One night after Bennie and Thelma had gone, Hal was sitting in his den, explaining mountain people to Yvonne.

"Civilization spreads out until it comes to a range of mountains. When it fills up, it begins to spill over. There are two groups who cross the mountains first. Each is a different racial mixture. The first group are the explorers, the ambitious go-getters. They're the adventurous bunch who have conquered the world. The best strains of the Andites. They git to the top of the mountains and they look out over all that virgin territory and all they see is opportunity. They don't even pause. They race out and grab all of it they can for themselves. They're excited and enthralled by the challenge." Hal eyed Yvonne as he lit a cigarette. "Are you interested in this?"

"Yes, yes, I'm listening. I'm excited and enthralled, like the Andites."

"The next bunch are fugitives. They're the more animal strains and they couldn't fit into society, couldn't make it where they were. They're in trouble one way or another. When they git to the top of the mountain and look out over all that empty space the fear hits them. The same fear that kept them from fitting into society where they was before." He got a long drag from the cigarette, "Instead of seeing all that opportunity and challenge and adventure, they see all the danger and strife and commitment. They hunker down right there on the mountain, cause they cain't go back. They breed in with one another and farm the rocky hillsides and quarrel among themselves. They're a fearful bunch and they'll kill you if you mess with 'em. An sometimes if you don't."

Yvonne was filing her fingernails. "Well isn't that just amazing?" She had a hard time putting up with his know-it-all pedantry.

During a period of several months, Benny gradually told Hal his life story. According to him, his father had been a guitar player and had, on occasion, played on the Grand Ole Opry. When Benny was thirteen years old, he had heard a man threaten to kill his father and he had borrowed an old double barreled twelve gauge shot gun, crept up on the porch of the man's shack, stuck the gun through the window and blew his head off.

They put Benny in jail, but "Big Jeff" got him out. Big Jeff had a hillbilly music band and his wife, "Tootsie," later became famous as the proprietress of "Tootsie's Orchid Lounge," a beer joint on lower Broad Street in Nashville. (Later, Hal would learn from Gene that the story about the shotgun and being in prison was all a story Benny had made up.) Benny was already a hell of a fiddler, and Big Jeff liked the boy and needed him in his group. It was during the Second World War and fiddle players got drafted like anybody else.

Genetically and environmentally, Benny was prepared for alcoholism, and when he began to taste the beer and moonshine whiskey in the honky tonks and backstages of central and east Tennessee, it dissolved the fear, guilt and home-sickness, and acted as a lubricant as he eased himself into the strange world inhabited by guitar players, club owners and promiscuous women. Hillbilly music became the boy's home and his schoolhouse, as he traveled the black top and dirt roads in a '38 Chevrolet, scrunched down in the back seat between a banjo player and a bull fiddle, breathing in the cigarette smoke and dirty jokes as he careened along the path that would lead him to the Grand Ole Opry and half of the jails in middle Tennessee.

For years Benny had heard the stories about Hal's drunken rampages in Music City, when he had terrorized some of the top people in the business, and he once told Yvonne that he had never been more surprised than when he met Hal and found him to be "so easy goin' and down to earth. I've never seen a man that was more talented than he is, but he don't make no big deal about it."

Benny was a fine songwriter himself and had written several big songs that didn't have his name on them and for which he never got paid. He would either sell them before they hit or put them in some wife or girlfriend's name because he was an exclusive writer for some publisher who he did not want to have the song. It was incomprehensible to Hal how someone with as great a talent as Benny or Carl Bellew could wind up without any money.

Of all the stories Benny told about Hank Williams, the saddest was one that happened in San Antonio, Texas.

Bill Monroe and his Bluegrass boys, Lester Flat and Earl Scruggs and several other acts were on the show. Hank was closing the show. No one could follow him.

Benny, who played fiddle for Flatt and Scruggs, was in the dressing room with Hank and they were sitting on cane-bottom chairs and drinking whiskey. Hank had on his pants, boots and hat, but only wore an undershirt over his bony chest. He had a fifth in each hand and would take a drink from one bottle and chase it with a drink from the other. He always had a cigarette between the first and middle fingers of his left hand and after each double drink, he would plaster the palm of his hand against his mouth and take a deep drag.

When Bill Monroe and his band came off, his banjo player left with a pretty fourteen year old girl who had been hanging around him all evening. Her father, who had brought her, came through the dressing room in a panic and asked Hank and Benny if they knew where the banjo player had "dragged his little girl off to." Hank took another double drink and another puff from the cigarette before he solemnly proclaimed, "I don't know nothin' about nothin', and there ain't nothin' I don't know nothin' about."

Hal believed that fear was the awareness of nothing, and the story about Hank reminded Hal of the prayer in "A Clean, Well Lighted Place," which began "Our Father who art in Nada, Nada be thy name."

Hemingway and Hank had both killed themselves, one with a shotgun and the other with whiskey. Each man left a beautiful description of the loneliness of man, cut off from God on a tiny planet near the edge of the universe.

Minnie Pearl had once asked, "Hank how could you be living this way when you wrote a great song like "I Saw The Light?" Hank answered with tears in his eyes, "Minnie, the truth is, there ain't no light."

Russell C. Skidmore, Coal Miner and Soldier, Retired Now

One mornin' in 1943
when the war was still on the
front page of the papers,
when there was frost on
the windshield of the car an
smoke comin' out
the kitchen chimney,
my Pa stepped out on the
porch with a Winchester
rifle and shot uncle Charlie
dead in our front yard.

Us kids were standin'
around by the mail box,
waitin' for the school bus to come.
Rachel busted out of the front
door screamin' and ran
past Pa and down into the
yard. She had a housecoat
over her nightgown an
she threw her self down on
top of Uncle Charlie's body,
screamin' an hollerin' an
holdin' his head in her hands.

Pa stood stock still
holdin' the rifle like he was
waitin' for a bird dog to flush
a covey of quail. No expression
on his face, just watchin'.
He said later he had
wanted to shoot Rachel, but he
couldn't git hisself to do it.

*   *   *

Old at last -
at last now, old -
aging eyes that saw
life inexorably unfold
devoid now of surprise
with a story very
much the same
as the ten-year soldier told,
no medal for bravery
no pension, no streets of gold,
a slow decrease in the amount
of blood that flows to the brain,
a slight limp,
and a shoulder that aches
when it rains.
A diminished capacity
for horror,
a cynic and a stoic
who expects nothing
from today or tomorrow,
but there is one memory
that strips away all the
veneer of torpor and toughness
and leaves me breathing
fast and hard,
when I think of the
morning when Pa
shot uncle Charlie
in our front yard,
when Pa shot uncle Charlie
in our front yard.

(Hal Bynum, Andite Invasion/BMI From the Album The Promise 2002)

So Little Of God and So Much Of The Other

That morning the aircraft came and I hid beneath a bridge
till they'd flown over to bomb somewhere else.
They were machines, not humans,
and when they were gone
and the fear subsided, it was as though they'd never been.

Among the dead under the shattered bridge was a middle-aged woman
with multiple wounds, making a harsh, gasping sound,
her eyes squinted shut with accepted agony.
I lifted her upper body and slid my lower body under hers,
propping her up.
Her arms fell loosely and her neck didn't work.

Suddenly her eyes flickered open and focused
on my face and neck and clothes.
She recoiled weakly in horror.
It must have been the blood.
I never knew how so much blood could come from an ear.
I had caught some shrapnel the night before.

I cleared my throat, which I hadn't used for a while and
searched for a comforting phrase,
"Would you like some bean dip?"

Her eyes widened in disbelief and shock
Then I saw her give up.
Her eyes skimmed over and she was suddenly dead in my arms.
I laid her gently in the mud and began to climb the slope.

They'd be here soon, dragging their worthless loot
and their damaged souls,
more victims than conquerors.

Chuck Howard, 1969

Chuck was lounging back in the swivel chair, his feet on Bobby Bobo's desk talking to Jim Kandy, "Son! You're the coldest mule I've ever tried to ride! What have you done to people in this town? They're all scared to death of you!"

Kandy chuckled happily, "I know it." He was stocky, balding and had a bright, intelligent look about him and had great, effortless presence. He sat very erect in the straight-backed chair cradling a motorcycle helmet under his right arm as though he were at parade rest in a police academy inspection, proud to serve and ready to die for the cause if necessary,

Hal studied him carefully. He seemed to be doing a parody on some type of individual that Hal was not familiar with. There was a joyful, wry cynicism about him and something down deep that constantly said, 'I don't give a damn, and as a consequence, I'm having a wonderful time. Life is a joke and I'm rising to the occasion,' or something like that. Hal liked him immediately.

Chuck was enjoying playing the role of the big executive about to fire an employee who has failed to fill the bill. He had cut a demo on Kandy and taken it to several record companies asking them for a budget so he could cut a big session that would adequately display Kandy's beautiful voice.

Chuck was digging vanilla wafers out of a box, chewing and talking with his mouth full. He was a diabetic. He shook his head sadly, "They all listened and nodded and listened and nodded and when the tape was finished, they all looked at me and said the same thing, 'How's the boy's mind?'"

Chuck's eyes wandered around the ceiling as though he were an electrical inspector about to condemn the wiring.

"How's the boy's mind?" He dug out a cookie and held it away from him, examining it from all angles. He suddenly dropped the wafer, lunged out of the chair, placed his palms on the desk and thrust his face toward Kandy, shouting, "How is your mind?!"

Everyone in the room roared with laughter. The acting and the timing were superb. Kandy beamed, he loved it.

Chuck lay back in the chair and laughed, "How's the boy's mind?"

When he had milked all the laughter there was going to be, he turned serious, "I'm gonna do it with my own money. Some people owe me, and some others I'll promise to pay 'em an never do it. Probably give the studio a hot check. It'll all work out." He pointed to Hal, "I want you to cut this boy's song. It's a great song. We'll do it instead of that dog of mine." He shook his head looking puzzled, "Now I'm knocking my own songs off the session. I must be going crazy. How's the boy's mind?"

Chuck picked Hal up in the afternoon before the night session. When

Hal got in the Cadillac, Chuck roared off, beginning to talk without any greetings.

"I called you early so we could stop by on the way and watch my boys play baseball. Chuckie's pitching an I ..."

"Baseball! Watch kids play baseball? Why in the hell — I could have rode with somebody else— why didn' you—"

"Cousin! Think what I'm doin' for you!" He was wearing a pale grey, three-piece suit identical to his powder blue one. He was waving his right hand as he drove, turning on the charm. "The little warrior does it again! Discovers starving unknown writer, hand-carries him to the very portals, I said the very portals of—"

"Chuck! I don't want to set and watch a goddamn ball game! I'm nervous as a son of a bitch. I been comin' off booze an I—" The tires squealed as Chuck whipped the car onto the freeway.

"Portals— I just got that word out of a book, portals," he roared on, deftly blocking Hal. "You know you need to teach me all those words you know. I never got to go to school. I need to know words. Reach out! Help the little diabetic! You could—would you look at that son of a bitch!" He passed a truck on the wrong side.

"Damn, Chuck!" The truck driver hit his air horn and Hal glanced around in time to see him shaking his fist.

"No sense of humor! The man's got absolutely no sense of humor. Ain't you glad we don't have to be around him all the time?" He reached out and gently gripped Hal's arm. Hal was still bracing himself against the dashboard. "Son, I tell you what, I'll stop an get you some beer, okay? Then you can settle down. A beautiful afternoon, a couple of beers and a ball game, now I ask you, what could be better? Then we'll roll on out to the barn and cut that old dog song of yours, alright?"

Hal remembered them stopping at a liquor store to buy a fifth of 180 proof grain alcohol, then stopping at a grocery store for cups and several bottles of Sprite. He remembered drinking and hollering and laughing with Chuck as they sat on some wooden bleachers and then he remembered nothing at all, no recording session, no ride home afterward, nothing. The first thing he knew it was early morning and he was lying on the bathroom floor, naked and sick.

Hal was sitting on the porch of the Clubhouse in the afternoon sunshine waiting for the new owner to open for business, when Chuck saw him, wheeled over and stopped. He got out of the car and walked slowly up the sidewalk. He sat down across the porch from Hal, staring thoughtfully and saying nothing. He had on the powder blue suit again.

Someone passed on the sidewalk and hollered, "Hi Chuck!" but Chuck gave no indication he heard, continuing to stare at Hal. When he finally spoke, his voice was tired.

"Well son, I guess you know what you've done to yourself in this town." Hal kept his face expressionless, but the bottom dropped out of his stomach. "Do you remember any of it?" His voice was cold. Hal shook his head, the tiniest of movements.

Chuck dropped his gaze to the floor of the porch, ran his hand through his thick brown curls and shook his head sadly, "My guess is, you're through in this town. A bunch of those musicians are producers. They were doing it for me as a favor."

He looked up at Hal again, his face deadly serious, "Everywhere I've been today people were talking about it."

Hal's stomach was in such a knot he could hardly breathe. He kept his face impassive.

"You don't remember any of it?"

Hal didn't respond. He couldn't go back to Fort Worth, nor Albuquerque either.

"It was the worst thing I've ever seen in this town." Chuck looked down the street and far into the distance, his hands resting on his knees.

"An I've seen a lot in this town, believe me." When Hal still didn't respond he continued, speaking softly, "At first people thought it was funny. If I could have got you in the car at that point—" his voice trailed off.

"The third time you kicked over Walter Hayne's guitar, you were through at Decca. George Richey was on piano, so you're through at Columbia." Chuck was opening and closing his hand slowly, staring at it as though he didn't know it would do that. "When you grabbed that little background singer, I thought her husband was going to hit you with a mike stand. It took four men to put you in the car and right in the middle of the next cut, you came bustin' in wantin' to fight everybody. You don't remember any of that?" When Hal didn't answer, Chuck stood up. For the first time Hal noticed how small he was. "You cost me between three and four grand. The tape's worthless." He turned and started down the steps, then stopped. He twisted his head slowly and looked back at Hal, "But that's not the worst part. The worst part is - - I lost a friend." Hal didn't turn his head to watch him, but he heard the car door close and heard Chuck drive slowly away.

After a while the man came and unlocked the front door, but Hal didn't hear him. He was leaning forward with his elbows on his knees, staring at the concrete.

Everything's Different Now

The sun shines in splashes on the soiled carpet
And old grey ashes in the fireplace
Clouds are runnin' from the wind
Back and forth and comin' back again
They're too few and far between
To hide the sun's face

It's a funny kind of day
I'm not unhappy cause you went away
It's just that everything's different
Everything's different now

You were kind of a fanatic
Everything had to be neat and clean
From the basement to the attic
Stuff I'd saved from childhood
Stuff I'd bought down below the border
It all had to be culled and sorted
Everything had to be put in order

I'm kinda like an old timber wolf
Beyond human rules and human reason
Suspicious of crowds and folks that talk too loud
Troubled and restless during certain seasons

Quick to anger, slow to forgive
Nobody could believe it when we first got together
A house was just a house to me
Roof and walls are all I need
A place to keep my belongings outta the weather
A hole to crawl into and sleep and read

Lookin' back, I can see you changed me a good bit
There's some pictures somewhere of me in funny clothes
You and me at a cocktail party, everybody smilin'
My hair slicked back on the sides
On your dress, you'd pinned a rose

But when the wind'd moan around the corner of the house
in the winter
We'd lay in front of the fireplace, eatin' chicken wings
And drinkin' beer
And you'd tell me how I wasn't as angry as I used to be
And how anyway, anger idn't always just a mask for fear

You always wanted me to tell you what I was thinkin'
But it was deeper than thinkin' an I couldn't put it in words
I'd always been lonesome and I guess after a while
You caught it from me
You spent more time in the backyard
Hummin' old songs an feedin' the birds

I'd wake up at night and you'd be sittin' and starin'
Like you was tryin' to memorize everything about me
And sometimes you'd go around the house
Just touchin' things
Like you was packin' some kind of a suitcase
I couldn't see

One morning I woke up and the door was wide open
Outside I could hear wild geese flying south
On my pillow was a paper without any writin'
Just some red lipstick where you'd carefully blotted your mouth

It's a funny kind of day
I'm not unhappy cause you went away
It's just that everything's different
Everything's different now
You came and you went and....
Everything's different now

(Hal Bynum, Andite Invasion/BMI From the Album It's My Time 1995)

At a Restaurant with Christopher

When Hal reprimanded the waitress and rejected the plate of fried eggs for the third time, Christopher ducked out of the booth without looking at Hal and said, "Dad, I'm going to the restroom."

Hal said, "Christopher, you just went to the restroom! You're just bored from waiting. You've got to learn to have patience!" He eased down slightly and said, "You cain't always have everything the way you want it right when you want it. You'll have to learn that."

The little eight year old boy glanced thoughtfully toward the kitchen and toward the table where the woman had set the plate each time and said nothing, obviously deep in thought.

Hal began to worry that Christopher would think he was being unfair. He explained, "That woman don't give a shit about her work. She wants to git back to that back table where she's sittin' with that other waitress and smoke cigarettes and talk against her daughter's husband and after awhile, when she gets her anger out, she can settle down and tell cute stuff her grandchildren say. Her husband's a truck driver and if she didn't need the money, she wouldn't goddamn be here."

Christopher's face was carefully inscrutable. He was not interested in the story. He slowly fingered one of the menus the woman had never picked up and gazed out the window.

When the tall woman banged the plate in front of him and walked away in a huff, Hal shook his head in disgust, "That still ain't over medium!" He looked for the salt and pepper. "Ta hell with it! I'll eat 'em anyway!"

The boy sighed with relief and turned his head back to gaze at the ceiling. He wouldn't look at Hal.

Hal hated eggs. He was eating them because he had a hangover and needed to steady his nerves and his stomach.

When they were half way across the parking lot, heading for the car, Christopher suddenly stopped, turned toward Hal, almost crying, "Dad! Do you just not care about people?!"

The man stood paralyzed. Christopher had never talked to him like that. "Well I - I don't know. I - guess I..."

He had never seen the child so distraught and disturbed, Hal felt like he had been hit in the pit of his stomach.

Christopher glanced around the parking lot and said. "Come on Dad, it's alright. Let's get in the car. People are watchin' us."

As they drove away, Hal's mind lurched from violent scene to violent scene, reliving a life of fierce encounters, groping for an answer to the boy's question. Something was wrong. Something had always been wrong. It was too much for him. It had always been too much for him.

He wanted to stop, put his head on the steering wheel and cry, but instead he turned and smoothed the blond hair and said weakly, "I love you, pretty boy."

Christopher said quickly, "Oh, I know it, Dad. It's okay."

A Lover's Prayer

Father, I ask you to forgive me for my lack of patience and for bein' self-centered an always thinkin' about myself and what I want, an wantin' to be comfortable all the time instead of tryin' to be a help to other people.

Most of all, I pray that you'll help me to always be gentle and good and understandin' with this woman who's chose to live her life with me. She loves me with all her heart, with a love that's innocent and trusting and unselfish.

You've had your hand on our lives since the day we met. We'd both been hurt a lot an neither one of us was ready to open our hearts again, but there was somethin' wonderful about that moment, almost like the world had conspired to place an emphasis on our meeting, when we came together that day.

I realized immediately how much she was.

There was this bright, burnin', knowin' in her eyes that cut right through her shyness and it was weird how we trusted each other, right from the start.

Whatever kind of carpet there was in that room caused an electric shock when our hands touched and we both laughed and it all got started in a relaxed an easy goin' way, an you brought us along, an brought us through everything that coulda wrecked us along the way.

Evertime I look at her I see the little girl who believes the world's a good place an everybody's got good in 'em, an that darkness is just a place the light hadn't got to yet.

Father, help me to trust you the way she trusts you. I want to have that kind of faith. No matter how bad things look, she believes if she does her best and tries hard enough, everything'll turn out alright.

Forgive me for bein' in such a hurry all the time an bein' worried when there idn't really any reason for it.

I think sometimes I look for the worst in people, tryin' to find somethin' wrong with 'em so I can feel better about me.

She's always lookin' for the good in people, an the funny thing is, she always seems to find it.

Help me to be as gentle, and thoughtful, and kind as she is. An to not always be makin' everthaing about me, to not always be tryin' to git everthaing the way I want it all the time.

She's the one that's taught me about kindness. An when I do remember to give a little bit of it back to 'er, when I remember to be thoughtful, she's so grateful that tears come to her eyes an she touches my face with her hand an I've never seen love like that.

I'll never understand why she loves me the way she does. Of all the gifts you've given me, that's the greatest gift of all. Help me to comfort her when she's troubled, and to somehow make her realize how beautiful and wonderful she really is.

I don't deserve her, but Lord, how I love her.
Help me to be good to 'er.
      Amen

(Hal Bynum, Andite Invasion/BMI From the Album, If I Could Do Anything 1998)

St. Louis, 1977 - Ft. Worth, 1954

On the way to the auditorium, as people chatted and the cars rolled along with the traffic, Hal let his mind flicker lightly over the problem of stage fright. So far he felt completely calm, but then that was how he had felt at the awards until the moment had come when they called his name and the orchestra hit "Lucille" and he was walking down the aisle. Then the adrenalin had exploded like a bomb into his blood stream. This time there wouldn't be sixty million people watching, he thought, looking out at the loading docks and warehouses they were passing on both sides.

Hillman Hall reminded him of a song Hal had written years before with a title neither of them could remember.

"It's something like 'The Palace in Dallas' or something like that. You remember, 'Say hello to Ruby, she's an old friend of mine.'" He sang the words and suddenly Hal remembered it.

"I don't know if that thing's any good. It seems to me like it wadn' all that good." Hal remembered sitting at the grand piano in the sunlit music room in the big old house on Cedar Lane and writing it in the key of 'D' to force himself to learn to play in D.

"I'm telling you man, it's a smash!" Hillman was chuckling, remembering the honky tonk song. "You could have a hit on it yourself. Think about it."

Hal had written it like it was in Dallas, but it was about people and bars he had known on Main Street in Fort Worth. He must have been nineteen or twenty years old. After a year at Texas Tech, in Lubbock, he had come to Fort Worth and worked a year or two, doing all kinds of jobs. In those days, the only place you could hear "hillbilly" music was in the worst beer joints in town. As they eased along in bumper to bumper traffic in downtown St. Louis, his mind was back in downtown Fort Worth, twenty-three years earlier.

The musician in the song was a fiddle player who lived with a waitress who worked in the Mountaineer Tavern. He played in the band at night and they lived in a room in the old hotel next door.

That part of Main Street was made up of old, run down hotels, pawn shops, liquor stores, dark bars, and greasy cafes with exhaust fans that blew the smell of frying hamburger meat along the sidewalks. Winos staggered along, plucking at sleeves and mumbling for money. At night the police patrolled in pairs, swinging long nightsticks and peering with slit eyes at the whores, pimps, two-bit con men and small time grifters.

Hillbilly music crashed out of the doors of the bars and men who worked at construction jobs in the day time prowled in and out of the bars, drinking beer and looking for women, or a fight. They wore white dress shirts, open at the neck with sleeves rolled up two turns. They had on pleated dress pants and perforated shoes and their dark tans stopped half-way up their foreheads. There were always some old people drinking up their old age pension checks and bumming drinks in the booths near the front door. The old women always seemed to be big and fat with some teeth gone, wearing shoes without laces on their sockless feet. When there was a good crowd at the bar and the band was playing, panhandlers would ease in and try to bum a drink before they were discovered and thrown out.

An old man named Billfold Bill peddled wallets and pocket watches. He was a pick-pocket and he liked to steal in one part of town and sell in another, but when he got drunk, he would forget and sometimes he was beaten up or arrested for trying to sell a man his own billfold.

Hal had first gone to the Mountaineer Tavern to see Willie Nelson. Willie was a disk jockey on KCNC and had an early morning show called "Wee Willie Nelson and His Milk Bucket Brigade." Hal woke up one morning, turned on the radio and suddenly the radio world of Hank Williams, Lefty Frizell, and Hank Thompson collided and integrated with the world of lesser reality which was Hal's life. The resulting crash left Hal as frozen and paralyzed as if another dimension had opened up.

KCNC was on East Fourth Street, almost out to Sylvania Drive. Hal was working for a finance company as a collector and was furnished a car to drive. It was a green 1954 Ford, and at that time it was new.

The front door of the radio station was locked and Hal pushed a doorbell button. The man came and after Hal told him what he wanted he said, "You want to see Willie Nelson. He does the early morning show. I'll go get him."

After a short wait, a thin young man with a shock of unruly brown hair opened the door. They shook hands and Hal told him he had helped write the song, "I'm Hot to Trot."

Willie seemed very pleased and impressed. "Both sides of the record are good, but that's the side I like best. I've been playing it more."

Hal said, "I wonder if I could – uh - see the record?"

Willie smiled, "Sure, I'll go get it."

Neither of them had asked him into the station. He waited on the steps, his heart pounding wildly.

When he came back Willie had a cold look on his face. "Whad you say your name was?"

"Hal Bynum!"

Willie looked at him and then looked away obviously embarrassed for Hal. "That's not the name it's got on it."

He handed Hal the record and under the song title it said "Gene Tabor." Hal held it with his fingers hooked through the hole, his thumb pointing up and shaking silently. He looked past the corner of the building at the light green spring leaves on the trees and bushes.

Hal suddenly saw a scene from a Saturday afternoon on the town square in the little town he'd grown up in. Some boys nine or ten years old were teasing a little boy about four years old. The older one was standing with his foot on the bumper of a car shaking his head and saying, "That's not your daddy's car."

The little boy was holding back the tears and saying over and over. "It is. It's our car."

Hal looked back at Willie and said, "Our names aren't on it."

Willie was embarrassed. He obviously didn't believe Hal was a writer on the song.

"You could call 'X' Records and tell them there's a mistake and they could correct it before they press any more of them." He took the record back. "Terry Fell's last record was 'Don't Drop It' so it should be a good record for him." He was watching Hal quietly, playing the thing out.

Hal said, "Thanks," and walked back down the sidewalk feeling sick, "You win it, and then you don't win it," he thought.

As he opened the door to get into the car, he saw that Willie was walking toward him. He stopped and looked across the top of the car at Hal. He had a different look on his face.

"You know, it wouldn't hurt to get in touch with them. Record companies put out corrections to radio stations ever so often, and like I was tellin' you, they could change it before they press any more of them." Something about the way Hal had taken it so hard and then just walked off, had convinced Willie he was telling the truth. Hal looked at him and it occurred to him there was something shy or bashful about Willie. He suddenly smiled warmly at Hal and asked, "Where are you from, anyway?"

They started talking and then walked around and sat on the front fender of the Ford, Willie twirling the record on his index finger from time to time and telling Hal what little he had been able to learn about the record business. He wrote songs too, and was working with Woody Woodward, area representative for Columbia Records, trying to get them recorded. Woody had a publishing company.

Before Hal left, Willie asked him to come down to the Mountaineer Tavern on Main Street where Willie was playing and singing at night.

When Hal was a child, his mother had sat at an upright piano in the old two story farm house and played and sung "Casey Jones" and "He's In The Jailhouse Now," and a light had lit up in his mind that burned brightly anytime he heard a song that told of real experiences in the lives of real people. He didn't get to hear one like that very often, but when he did the light would flare up and burn again. He used the light like bio-feedback, following wherever he had to go to keep it burning, and it led him straight into the steel guitar whining, juke box thumping, honky tonk world of country music.

Two Women

Let me tell you about two women.

One was an old lady I visited a few days ago in Albuquerque, New Mexico. She sits in a lawn chair under the carport where she can see people goin' down the street and wave to 'em as they go by. She's deaf and can't hear the birds anymore, but she watches 'em and makes little clucking noises, which they ignore, and of course, the people in cars don't wave back. They're in too big a hurry.

Her daughter cooks for her and there's a woman who comes in twice a week to bathe her and doctor her skin problems. She has a cat that follows her everywhere and sleeps in her lap. In the evenings she watches T.V., but she can't hear the sound.

She remembered me, and I asked her a question she didn't hear, and she answered by telling me how she was recoverin' from two broken arms which were gradually gittin' better. I knew she hadn't never broken her arms, but I examined the places she pointed to.

She can't make quilts anymore - and her eyesight's too poor to read.

When my wife and I drove away, she was standin' under the carport, not realizin' we were leavin'.

I remember another woman, young and strong and solid and pretty. She taught school in West Texas and raised two children and worked in the field, choppin' cotton and diggin' up Johnson grass.

I remember her in the back yard, under a clear blue Texas sky, her feet apart and her mouth in a straight line as she wrung a chicken's neck, her dark hair flyin' around and the white feathers flyin' around.

She'd skin the chicken, rinse it in cold water, salt and pepper it, dust it in flour and fry it in a pan of hog lard.

Summer in West Texas: fried chicken with white gravy, biscuits, mashed potatoes and fried ochra.

She would work all day in the hot sun and in the evenin' she'd read a book to the girl and the boy, holding it toward a coal oil lamp, her voice ringin' strong and clear in the old wooden farm house.

The bible — and church — and clean clothes — and warm beds in the winter — and a cool wash rag for a child's forehead when he had a fever.

An endless supply of energy, a strong jawed certainty about how good people ought to live - and a constant one-woman war against poverty and sin.

It's hard for me to realize both of those women are — the same woman. A wife who is now a widow, a parent who is now a little child again.

She taught me to walk, she taught me to read, she taught me to work — and how to keep goin' when life gets rough. The way it's rough for her now.

And I just realized, she's the one that taught me to Love.

An I do love her — my mother.

(Hal Bynum, Andite Invasion, BMI From the Album, The Promise, 2002)

Full Circle

Ever since the man had slumped over the steering wheel and passed out, the little boy had been alone in the world. He was afraid to get out of the car. It might be the wrong thing to do, and if it was, the man would find out about it later and beat on the child's body with his hand.

The west Texas town had red brick streets and the boy could see people moving around in some of the stores. It was mid afternoon on a warm spring day and everybody but Hal knew what to do. He looked back at his father, snoring and snorting and from time to time moaning in his sleep. Hal wished somebody would come out to the car and take care of them.

Finally, he felt so lonely and unsafe he opened the door of the car, and after a slight hesitation he stepped down into the street. He stood with one hand on the outside handle and looked up and down the sidewalk, searching for kindness. A man wearing a once white western hat stood in a doorway, chewing a toothpick and squinting at the day.

Hal came up close and asked the man, "Would you help my daddy and me? Would you help us get home?"

The squinted eyes moved to the car and studied the scene briefly before returning to the boy. He took the toothpick from his mouth. "Where do you live?"

For the first time Hal wanted to cry. "I don't know."

"You don't know where you live?"

Hal thought of the old ranch house and the porch and his dog, Prince. "My grandmother's there."

The man studied Hal for a moment, "How old are you?"

Hal glanced down the street. Maybe he needed to find someone else.

"Four. I'm four years old." He felt vaguely ashamed that he wasn't older and bigger. He knew he needed to be.

Further down the street a woman had stepped out of a door to examine the situation and Hal began to move toward her. He had given up on the man. He took a couple of steps and then stopped and turned back to face him again.

"You won't tell the sheriff will you?" Hal looked at his father, helpless in the car. "The sheriff will take him away. They'll put him in jail."

When the man made no response, Hal turned and walked toward the woman. She had begun to move in his direction, a look of concern on her face.

Many years later, Hal sat at a glass topped table on the patio behind his brick, ranch styled home in Green Hills, a rich suburb of Nashville, and tried to remember how he had gotten home that spring afternoon in Spur, Texas. The memory shut off at the place where he began to tell his story to the woman. That was the end of it.

Hal poured himself another drink of whiskey and lit a Pall Mall, gazing at the big back yard. Earlier in the day he had been reading a book that had reminded him of that scene in Spur. It told how it was the father's role and responsibility to take a son out into the world and introduce him to life, and life to him, and to let the child see the father interact with society. Kind of like the way an animal teaches a pup how to hunt.

He took a long drink from the glass and thought about his collision with life— his "man against the system" mentality, and how his career could have been a parade, but he had chosen to make it a battle rather than fit in and adjust to the way big business does business.

He took another drink. "Maybe you just loved the drama of the thing." And then after a moment, "Or, maybe it's just cause that's all you've ever known."

He went over and hid the bottle among the plants that grew along the brick wall of the patio. In a few minutes Cynthia would be bringing Christopher over for the weekend and he didn't want her to know he was drinking.

Love at First Sight and Forever

Sometimes at night, sittin together on the couch, watchin' T.V. to get the day's business out of our minds, you'll mute the sound and turn toward me, pullin' my head down so you can kiss me, and then you'll say,
   "Tell me again how I looked to you that first day you saw me."

You'll have a kind of playful look on your face, but in your eyes I see a look of thankfulness that we got together, and a look of hunger to relive that moment, which you know means as much to me as it does to you.

So I tell you what all you wuz wearin' that afternoon, 'cause I know you don't like for the story to end right away, an how your long, dark hair looked in the sunshine, an how you was wearin' socks without any shoes on out in the yard no matter what your folks had taught you when you was a kid. We both just stood there lookin' at each other, kinda stunned or somethin' an for a little bit of time, neither one of us said a word.

You were a mature woman, but you had a little girl look about you, an eyes that were ready to laugh, but neither of us was laughin'. We were both off-balance and surprized. Lookin' back, I still cain't figger out what happened right then, but it was profound an it hit us both the same way.

We both kind of kept each other at arms length for awhile cause it was a little bit scary, somethin' we couldn't understand takin' ahold of us an throwin' us around like that.

With me it was sumpm' about bein' in control. I'd always had to be in complete control in relationships, an I could tell this was different and I didn't know how to deal with it.

We were both involved with other people, but my mind was on you most of the time, an you told me later, it was the same with you. As I got to know you, I could see that there was a whole nother world openin' up to us and that there was a life waitin' for us that would be new an different from anything either of us had ever experienced before.

For once, I didn't make a move. But then you did. You were shy, but you had the courage to do it, an I never quit bein' grateful to you for that.

Our life's been kind of a roller coaster ride, but we've both been happy ever day an ever day I've prayed I could be more like you. Your goodness always amazes me. When I hear the word, "sincerity," I always think of you.

We're always workin' together, or laughin together, or plannin' together, an bein' with you has helped me to grow up enough to where I believe I could face anything that might happen - - - except havin' to live without you.

I've never found anythaing about you I don't like. You're a lot of thaings, an one of 'em is a little girl that don't know how beautiful you are. Ever time we git fixed up to go out somewhere, you always ask me, "Are you sure I look alright?" an I laugh an tell you again that you do.

I always want to give you everthaing I ever can, an I know before too long you'll look up at me an say,
    "Tell me again how I looked to you the first time you saw me."

An I will.

(Hal Bynum, Andite Invasion/BMI From the album The Promise 2002)

A Leap of Understanding

I didn't git a whole lot of schoolhousin', and whatever they teach in them big colleges about different cultures and diverse racial customs is all a mystery to me, but I grew up out on the barren, windswept West Texas plains where the American Indian had made his livin' and fought his fights and raised his children since before recorded time, and when my people, who were frontier people, moved into the land and started raisin' crops and livestock and a different color of kids, there was bound to be a hell of a commotion.

That adjustment has at times required gunfire, house-burnings, cavalry charges and kidnappin's on both sides. It was pretty much worked out by the time I came along, but there was still the feelin' of strangeness between the two peoples, and anything approachin' a close relationship required what you might call, I guess, a leap of understanding.

When I was sixteen years old, my dad took me a day's drive down south into central Texas. He wanted me to see where he had grown up in Coryell County. My grandad had broke horses and mules for the Wallace ranch and when my dad was a boy, they lived in a rock house beside a creek that had cottonwood and sycamore trees growing along its banks. The house was still standin', although the doors and windows and part of the roof was gone. We stood in the front room, and he showed me openings, down low in the wall, where men could lie on the floor and fire rifles durin' indian raids. His uncle, Elijah I. Bynum, was killed along the Washita River by a bunch of renegade Comanches.

On my mother's side of the family, my great grandmother's life was saved by a band of indians. They were friends of the family, and one afternoon, when they stopped to water their horses and visit, they found she was being held hostage by a drunken, runaway slave with a butcher knife. The rest of the family had gone into town to get supplies. They'd left the old woman there because she had just gotten over influenza and was too weak to ride in a wagon.

The indians killed the slave and scalped him and buried him in a gully about a hundred yards behind the house.

Later on, after I was a grown man, I had a job as a caseworker for the welfare department in northern New Mexico. There was an old man named John Cayatano who lived on the reservation near the trading post. I liked him a lot and I'd stop by and visit with him from time to time. John could speak Spanish. It had been a tradition for the fathers to pass it down to the sons. That had all started back when the Spanish soldiers captured the little Navaho boys and make 'em work at the missions. When they were grown, they'd turn 'em loose and git new ones. I never learned much Navajo, but John and I could do alright in Spanish. The only English words I ever heard him say were the names of towns.

One winter night we were talking in his hogan and I was sweatin' as usual, 'cause they always kept the tin stoves red hot, and John and me were squattin' on our heels on the dirt floor, the women folk sittin' on the ground the way they always did, wrapped up in wool blankets. A hogan is a small, round mound made outta cedar posts and mud with only one low entrance and a hole in the top for the stove pipe to poke out of. There was a mattress that took up about a third of the room, but nobody was sittin' on it. A gasoline lantern gave off a yellow light and our bodies made dark shadows on the mud walls.

After a short silence, John said, "You know, I went to Washington one time."

I looked surprised, and he explained that back in the Depression, the Bureau of Indian Affairs chose he and his family to take to Washington and make pictures with the big shots so they could publicize what they were doing for the Indians. He told his wife to see if she could find the pictures.

While she was looking, I asked him, "So what did you do while you were there?"

He said, "Nothing. I stayed at the house of a crippled gringo. That's all."

I said, "Who was he?"

John shrugged, "I don't know, a crippled gringo. He had a wife. They were the people I stayed with."

When he handed me the picture, I saw John and his wife and Franklin D. Roosevelt in a wheelchair, and standing beside him, Eleanor.

I guess in racial matters, a leap of understanding is probly needed on both sides.

(Hal Bynum, Andite Invasion/BMI From the Album If I Could Do Anything 1998)

Johnny Dollar and the Meat Cleaver

Hal said, "One of the worst things I ever got into was one time when Dollar was crazy drunk on Tequila and went for me with a meat cleaver in an Albuquerque radio station. It was on a Saturday afternoon and the only people in the station were Dollar and me, and two advertising salesmen that had been drinking with him. Dollar had the idea I had told his old lady about him bangin' a Mexican girl and the more tequila he drank, the more he kept crowding me."

Hal saw the scene again; the desert sun streaming in through the glass front of the radio station, the row of desks and the leather roller chairs cluttering and blocking his passage to the back door, the hat rack he never managed to get a hold of. "Them salesmen were both buddies Dollar had brought in from Odessa, once he had got in good with Walter Styles, who was running KARA then, and we'd all been playing poker for several hours. Dollar had completely automated the station. Everything was taped; spots, records, whatever, so that nobody had to be there. Dollar was trying to cheat, but he was too drunk, and we'd caught him at it two or three times, and he was getting madder and crazier from the tequila, and when I won the pot that broke him, he started cussin' me and brought up that thing about his wife. By then I was sick of the whole thing, (I wasn't drinking at that time) and I suggested if he didn't like it, he might could shit in his hat and wear it awhile, so as to take his mind off of it.

"He was over in the little kitchenette, pourin' himself another drink and there was a big shiny meat cleaver layin' on a cuttin' board with some lemons he'd been cutting and he grabbed it and made a dive for me, bellerin' and screaming and swinging that cleaver."

Hal felt the hair stand up on the back of his neck as he saw the scene again. Dollar's face had gone chalk white and spit was running from the corner of his mouth as he roared through clenched teeth.

"I rolled over one of those glass-topped desks and he hit right behind me. Pieces of glass flew all over the office and I just had time to git up and grab one of the roller chairs before he leaned across the desk and swung at me again. He hit the back of the chair that time, and I tried to keep it between me and him, but I didn't have that much strength, on account of I had amoebic dysentery I'd caught down in Mexico and I only weighted a hundred and thirty-five pounds. He yanked the chair out of the way with his other hand and I had a shot at his jaw but I didn't have my feet set and I knew as light as I was, I was gonna have to nail him with everything I had.

Them other boys were behind him and could have grabbed him but they were standing there with their mouths open. One of 'em still had his cards in his hand. I back pedaled and he missed me by a few inches and the cleaver sunk into a metal filing cabinet and that time I had my feet under me and I cross-stepped and hooked him on the button of his chin with my left hand. I got every pound I had into it and he spun clean around with his back to me and fell on his face. His arms and legs twitched a couple of times and then he laid there like he was dead. I was so weak, I couldn't put the boots to him.

"Them other fellers were still standin' there and as soon as I had the breath, I said, 'You yellow bellied bastards! I ought to come after you with that cleaver!' They both hit the front door and I finally had to load Dollar in his car and take him out to my folks' house and let him sleep it off. I didn't know where he lived."

After a Scrape

When the ones that had got killed were buried
and the mess was all cleaned up
When the guns and the gun belts was all
loaded with catridges again,
when we'd all drunk us some whiskey and eat some supper,
The old man that was our leader
come and squatted down beside me
with his back to the fire.
He said, "Son, it don't look like it
but we're makin' a country,
a nation you might say
an someday they'll write about it
in books an they'll give the
names of the places and the dates
when it all happened, an
people'll flip through the pages, later on
an it'll sound like it was always gonna happen that way
they may ebm' tell it like it was easy
But the blood on our clothes
and the stench in our nose
an the achin' empty feelin'
you're feelin' right now
is a testament to the awful truth -
that it never was easy
and it never seemed sure to God sure
An I may sound a little shaky
after what happened today
but there's times I can't keep from thainkin'
By God, it could still go either way."

He stood up slowly
lookin' off into the darkness,
and then, almost in a whisper,
"Shit house mouse, it shore got rough
fer awhile there today."

Christmas Party, 1974

It was at a Capitol Records Christmas party in 1974 and Hal was smoking dope and arguing with a new man in the sales department. He decided to take the slack out, jerk the man's chain. He saw Bunter and the Kid grinning at each other and waiting for it to come.

"What the hell you mean I don't know anything about you? All you sales people have got the same story. You started out as a disk jockey in Portland, Oregon readin' the morning news and doin' a Sunday mornin' gospel program and before you could say 'Jim Ed Brown' you were doin' the Bumper to Bumper show and screwin' the P.D.'s old lady. That's what got you fired and you worked for a couple of years in top 40 until Shelby Singleton discovered you and brought you to Nashville. Now you're in sales and you've switched wives and you're playing golf and gettin' drunk at Bandy's and makin' a fool of yourself. You've got some yokel you're tryin' to get on the label and when he gets rollin' you're gonna be his manager. Then you can switch wives again and snort some coke. Catch the phone there, it's your mother on line two."

He turned and walked back to the hors d'oeuvres as the room exploded with laughter.

Meeting In Reno

I came to Virginia City before there ever was a Nevada. When they discovered that big vein of silver ore they called the Comstock Lode, I made a killin' sellin' tents and Mexican burros, and I built the Palace, the finest gamblin' hall this side of San Francisco.

Man, that was a whole nother world. You cain't imagine what it was like. The town was on the boom and silver ran through the Palace like a river and I was rich over night. As I sit here in this boardin' house, livin' on church charity and waitin' for the end, I can still hear the sound of cards and dice an women's voices, screamin' with laughter, and gunfire in the streets.

But, all along it was my destiny to wind up like this, without a dime an no way in the world to do anythaing about it.

An if there's one thaing I know and believe with all my heart, it's that there ain't no way in the world that a man can escape his destiny, no matter how he tries or what he does.

I learned that from a gambler that worked for me in the Palace.

He was a cold-eyed man with ice water in his veins, and his hands were like lightnin', whether they were handlin' cards or a pistol.

I didn't think there was any use in killin' as many men as he did, but he made me a lot of money and when it came to money, I was always in a hurry.

He was a lot different when I first hired him. He was kind of an innocent young feller back then. All he wanted to do was be free from workin' like a slave, plowin' corn from daylight till dark ever day of his life.

The money and the pistol bought him freedom from hard work an livin' on corn bread and sow-belly, but once he got hooked on that easy money and the power of the gun, he couldn't let go of it.

He came into my office one day, an all that cold, hard, mean look was gone, and his face was white as a sheet and his hands were shakin'.

In a quiverin' voice he told me to open the safe where he kept his sack of money so he could buy the fastest horse he could find and flee to Reno. I poured him a big drink of whiskey and made him sit down an tell me what had happened to 'im.

He said he had been walkin' around the town square, waitin' for the cigar store to open, and he'd bumped into an old woman wearin' a long black robe with a hood over her head.

When he looked inside the hood, he saw that it was death and the expression on her face when she saw him caused the cold hand of terror to close around his heart.

After I give him his money and he bought a horse and spurred down the street, headin' for Reno, I walked to the town square and right away I spied the hooded figure.

I looked into the face of death and as soon as I could get my breath again, I said,
"Why'd you wanna scare my dealer?"

And death spoke sayin',
"I didn't mean to frighten him. I was just surprised to see him here.
"I'm supposed to meet him tonight in Reno."

(Hal Bynum, Andite Invasion/BMI From the Album If I Could Do Anything 1998)

Marigold, 1981

Marigold sat cross-legged on the carpeted floor of her office, a manila folder of correspondence lying open in front of her.

"Bynum, I don't have time for an alcoholic rehabilitation program! Can't you see that? This office is just——" She swept her hands out in an expanding gesture that began at her bosom and ended with her arms widely outspread. She imitated the sound of an explosion. "People are in and out o' here like — ants! I've just come back from two weeks in England. What a high that was!" She straightened her back and turned her head majestically, peering at him over the half-lensed reading glasses.

"Bynum, they entertained me like Royalty!" She held the posture and gazed at him with defiance for a moment then relaxed and shook her head tiredly, gesturing toward the closed door that led to the outer office. "You wouldn't believe what goes on in here." She pulled the glasses off and let them hang from the silver chain that went around her neck. She had on Levis, cowboy boots and a tailored western shirt.

She tightened her lips, leaned toward him and whispered loudly, "I've got five Italians out in that back office! They're gonna be here three weeks. I'm the only one who can write checks for them! God! Would you believe it?"

She relaxed, slumped her shoulders and nodded sadly at the floor, assuming an attitude of exhausted resignation. She cocked her head to the side and slowly looked up at him with a sad smile.

Hal felt uncomfortable. He uncrossed and re-crossed his legs behind the little white coffee table and tried to think of a way to bring her back to reality. It was hard to do when she was at the office.

She reassumed the tired resignation and said humbly, "I don't know what I'm doing. I don't know how it all fits in. I just do God's will." She gestured weakly toward the ceiling. "That's all any of us can do."

Hal leaned forward on the little love seat, putting his elbows on his knees and pushing his hat back with a quick movement of his thumb. "Marigold, you've got to get into a group where all you are is your soul. Where you aren't a big songwriter, or a world traveler, or a big shot publisher, or somebody with a lot of money or—where you're just what you are at that moment. One little bitty person searching for the Truth. A tiny grain of sand in the universe. Not,——" He glanced around the room at all the awards and pictures of Marigold with famous people, — "Daytona Beach."

She had put the glasses back on while he was talking and she looked at him over the tops of the lenses, holding a letter picked from the folder of correspondence. "Bynum, you just don't know all I've got to do. All the people I've got depending on me. The house. You won't have all the time you've got now, when you get your house. You just won't."

"Marigold," he said, leaning closer to her, "It's not the time. You've got the time. That's not it and you know it." He looked at her face, taut with strain. "You'll have more time if you do." He leaned back. "An it'll be better time."

She dropped the letter back into the folder and laid the glasses back on her shirt-front.

"Bynum, I'm not worried about my soul. My soul's not what's wrong with me, I'm just exhausted. I need to spend some time with God, at the piano. That's when I feed my soul, praising him at my piano. It just all comes out."

Hal leaned forward again, "Marigold, this is a program of ego deflation and that's what I use it for. I have to. Every day. To get my self out of the way so God can work through me and I can grow." He motioned to the door. "All that drama out there is just a way of making the story about you instead of about God. You remember, I used to always be tellin' you how you needed to work with little kids so you'd have to get out of yourself. With little kids you've got to get down on their level." He hurried on, trying to get as much of it in as he could before she exploded. "They don't know nothin' about fame an reputation and influence. They just know about Love. They know that's the best stuff they ever git, an they like it a lot. Who you are don't mean nothin' to them. They see your soul. Probably see that aura you talk about. Who knows?"

The explosion came. "Bynum! I worked with kids for years! I was a freakin' school teacher, remember?" She ran her hands through the short-cropped hair. "Jesus! Don't you see that all that's wrong with me is I'm exhausted!?" She began to relax a little and then looked around for her cigarettes. They were on the coffee table. She took one from the little case that looked like a coin purse and then fumbled her lighter out.

Hal leaned back again and let the breath go out of him. He realized she wasn't ready. All he could do was love her and wait for the world of unreality to fall in on her. He felt tired. "Kid said you got drunk the other day."

The blood drained from her face and she sat frozen, the smoke still in her lungs and the lighter still aflame. After a moment, her eyes left his face and she put the lighter back in the little purse, blowing the smoke toward the floor. She turned her head back toward him and said with shaky defiance, "Yeah, I did! How about that?!" She guffawed and took another deep drag from the cigarette. "I let it all hangout. Got all that out of my system!" Her color had come back and there were red splotches on her face and neck. "I hadn't eaten anything all day and I drank some champagne it hit me like a ton of bricks."

She was up on her knees now, very erect, sitting on the heels of her boots. She reached out to the ashtray on the coffee table and ran the cigarette slowly around the rim, turning it as she went, paring and trimming the ash. Her face was harder when she looked up at him and her eyes were narrow. "You know we seem to have to do that from time to time."

He didn't bother to parry the thrust. "Kid was worried about you, that's how come he told me about it." He felt bad about breaking Kid's anonymity.

"That's good. That's good that he was," she nodded making an effort. "That's a big step for him."

Hal thought about taking off his jacket but decided he would be leaving soon. He lifted his hat off instead, dropping it on to the knee of his crossed leg. He ran his hand over the top of his bald head to see if it was sweating. It was.

"Yeah, well, he's worried about his own drinkin'. He's mentioned a couple of times that he might like to come to a meeting. I don't know if he will or not." Hal stood up. There wasn't anything he could do. Marigold stood up too, facing him.

"I'm the only one who can make it all happen! Denmark! Sweden! Belgium! And now Italy! Would you believe it?!" She did her crazy cackling laugh.

Her mood suddenly swung and dipped as she said angrily, "And Bart!" She took a deep drag from the cigarette. "I had no more than got off the plane than Bart was on my case. 'You're not a mother to me!'" She was imitating a whining child, twisting her beautiful face into ugliness.

"He kept doing that until I had to threaten him with you. My God! I don't know what I'd do if he wasn't scared shitless that you'd tear his arms and legs off."

Hal thought of the big, fat, foul smelling man, whining for the mother who hadn't been there when he was little and pretty. A wave of compassion washed away the revulsion he always felt when he got close enough to Bart to catch his rank smell or see the loneliness in his eyes. "God, help us on this dark little planet!" he thought.

She guffawed again, "After I threatened him with you, Neal an I came home that night and he had the door chained. When he let us in, I asked him why he had the door chained and he said, 'In case Hal came over.'"

"Neal told him, 'If Bynum wanted in here, that door wouldn't stop him.'" She laughed the laugh again.

Hal shook his head sadly, thinking of the legacy of fear his drinking days had left in the town. Hal Bynum, the Boogerman. The Boogerman will get you. He moved toward the door. She moved over and gripped his arm.

"Bynum, I have to talk to you ever so often." Her eyes were wide and soft now, defenseless. The poses and stances were all gone. "I knew that's what I was needing. I get something from you I don't get from anyone else. You're the only one who doesn't want something from me!"

Hal looked at the woman who had brought him to God so many years before and he was suddenly full of love for her.

"Marigold, tell me how I can help you. I love you enough to. I want to bad enough."

She dropped her eyes and a tear ran along the side of her nose. They stood there for a few moments and then she let go of his arm and wiped the tear off, shaking her head slowly.

"I'm just exhausted. I just need some time alone with God. At the piano." She turned to put the cigarette out and he opened the door and walked down the hall toward the parking lot, digging for his keys.

The Strange Disappearance of Lyla

Down at the Burger King, they tell me everything
They say that Lyla came back for a while
OOO, OOO, OO, OO, OO, OO
They say she came back for a while

The pigeons all looked down on Robert E. Lee
A statue of bronze beneath a magnolia tree
She hung her raincoat on the tip of his sword
And we sat drinkin' wine on the hood of her old Ford

I heard it secondhand, and I still don't understand
They say she had lunch with a priest
OOO, OOO, OO, OO, OO, OO
They say she had lunch with a priest

They say they saw her, but I don't believe it
I'm still keepin' her puppy - she'd never leave it
I think they're all mistaken somehow
Anyway, he's a great big ole dog now

She had that hippie look, she read all them yogi books
But sometimes she's cry in the night
OOO, OOO, OO, OO, OO, OO
Sometimes she'd cry in the night

Down at the Burger King, they tell me everything
They say that Lyla came back for a while
OOO, OOO, OO, OO, OO, OO
They say she came back for a while

(Hal Bynum, Andite Invasion/BMI From the Album The Promise 2002)

Chuck Howard, 1983

For months Hal had known Chuck was dying. Ever since the last time Haggard had recorded in Nashville, Chuck had been going down hill fast. Chuck was broke at the time and he had decided to sell Merle on the idea of having Chuck go on the road with him and open his shows. Merle didn't need anyone to open his shows, but Chuck needed the money and it would give him a chance to exert more influence over the songs Haggard recorded.

Hal said, "Damn, what a you want? He cuts everything you pitch 'im."

"Cuts? What he cuts doesn't matter. It's what gets released, you know that! Son, that man's got more stuff in the can than——."

He turned in the booth and opened the attaché case he always carried, or had somebody carry for him. He picked out a round plastic case, laid it on the table and opened it. There were different colored pills in each little pie-slice compartment and he selected a yellow tablet and popped it into his mouth, washing it down with coffee. "Gotta perk up, son, gotta perk up." The Percodan opened up his veins and when he ran the caffeine in the coffee against it, it gave him the energy to get around, and the power he needed to roll his show. The show was a weak version of what it used to be, but it was still an amazing phenomenon and unparalleled in the annals of human behavior. The timing was still there, the acting was superb and the wit was incisive and unfailing.

Hal looked at the little, scrawny, blood-starved body inside the western clothes, mustache and cowboy hat that looked as strange and incongruous on him as the capped teeth he had had for the last year. Chuck in his cowboy suit. Until he opened the attaché case, you figured he had a pair of leather chaps and some spurs in it.

Chuck leaned back and studied Hal for a few seconds before he put the case back on the seat beside him.

"There's two things we've got to do. We've got to get the deal-killers out of the way. I'll take care of that. The other thing, you've got to do. You've got to get with Merle and hit him with the fact that I'm loyal. 'Chuck's a team player, etc.' You can do it. He trusts you." He took a drink of the coffee.

"Chuck, why should he believe me? I've never done any business with him!"

"He likes you. He's always talkin' about you. He thinks you're a genius." Chuck turned hard. "You don't wanta do it. Is that it?"

Hal dug his cigarettes out. "I just don't think all that intrigue is necessary. You work a lot harder'n you need to. You tend to con yourself in and then keep connin' til you've conned yourself out the other side. Besides,—" Hal lit the cigarette and then stared at the lighter in his hand, "I'm not sure he listens to what I say. I think he's mostly puttin' up with me."

Chuck leaped forward in the booth and grabbed Hal's left arm, a savage look on his face.

"Will you listen to me?!! Will you listen to me for once in your life?!!"

Hal glanced around the restaurant, checking to see how many people were watching the wild little man with the loud voice.

"Don't look to see who's watching us! You afraid of bein' embarrassed? I'll really embarrass you. I'll jump up on this table and take my dick out! Listen to me!!" He gripped Hal's forearm harder. Suddenly he stopped and gave Hal a piercing and penetrating look. "Ah, I see." He released his grip and leaned back, "I see. You're dancin' so I'll tell you all the things he says about you." He shook his head with disgust, "Son, will you ever grow up and quit trying to feed your pore old ego? You don't need that. My God, son, you've got it all and don't know it. When you're sober and straight, nobody's got a chance. My God! Don't you know that?!" Chuck suddenly softened and reached out to grip his forearm again, gently this time. He gave Hal his sad and beseeching look and said in a voice close to a whine, "Don't make me have to reassure you every time we start to do some little piece of work!"

Hal was pretending to stare at the catsup bottle in order to irritate Chuck, but he was watching the little man with his peripheral vision and enjoying the act. It was superb.

Chuck ducked his face down and got between Hal and the catsup bottle.

"Look at me son, I'm dyin', we both know that. It ain't no big deal, it happens all the time. But—!!" Hal had fixed his vision on Chuck when he had started talking about dying and Chuck had moved his face to the side and upward so that he was sitting straight up again and Hal was watching him. "But before I go, I'd like to get in shape to leave something for my kids. And in the process," he leaned back in the booth, slumping a little, obviously worn out after the tirade, " — in the process, get you back rolling again. You're locked out in this town and you know it. You've got to get hot again and I can do it for you. All the doors are closed to you. They're afraid of you. They're all afraid you'll kill 'em. It's as simple as that. Gimme a cigarette. I'm gonna smoke a cigarette. To hell with 'em all! But don't tell Kathy." He grabbed the cigarette. "And don't tell George Richey, I've got a hundred dollar bet with him."

Hal lit the Pall Mall for him and he took a long drag, holding the cigarette out and studying it as though he were doing a T.V. commercial.

"Who are the deal killers?" Hal interrupted. You had to keep the left jab in Chuck's face. If you let him get his feet set he'd pound you out of the ring.

"You know who they are. _____ and _____. I've got everybody else wired. Tex is on my side." He blew a layer of smoke onto the tabletop and watched it rise. "Of course they're all out to get him too. He knows that. And Fuzzy, I've had all along. The joker in the deck. You taught me that a long time ago."

Hal nodded, "Yeah, I told _____ that years ago when he was running Merle's company, or whatever he was doin'. He spent a half a day telling me how he had it all rolled up and all the stuff he was gonna be running and controllin': an I sat there in that office he had in the U.A. Tower and listened to all that onslaught of ego and facile, pseudo wisdom, an when he got through I said, '_____, you're gonna be out on your ass in a matter of months, or maybe even weeks, and it's gonna be because of one mistake you're makin'. You're overlooking and underestimatin' Fuzzy. He's the joker in the deck. Sooner or later you're gonna play a hand and come up against him, and when you do, you're gonna lose. You'd better work with him. Don't try to go around him, it won't work. He's a good guy and he can be your ally.' As you know he didn't listen."

Chuck nodded, "And he was out on his ass." He stopped the waitress as she passed their booth. "Honey, would you bring me a bowl of strawberries with a little milk in the bowl. Just enough to cover the strawberries." He looked at her pleadingly. "Don't charge me for a whole glass of milk. Help a dying man. Reach out." When she left, he turned back to Hal.

"I've taken care of _____ and _____. They did it to themselves. I don't want to go into all the details but basically what happened was, _____ cut this old dog album on _____ and couldn't do anything with it, so I went to Merle, got him to sing on it, got him to finance it and then I sold it to Capitol for fifty grand; probably my most brilliant stroke. Went through Steve Stone. Pulled it off. Couldn't be done. I did it. Give me another cigarette. In the process, _____ and _____ beat Merle out of sixteen grand." He held the Pall Mall and motioned for Hal to light it.

"Okay —the album was a piece of shit and never came out. So — now here's where it gets interesting. During Merle's bass fishing tournament at whatever lake that is he lives on—"

"Lake Shasta."

"Whatever. During that tournament, they flew out there, got with Merle and told him he still owed _____ ten grand."

"Are you kiddin'?"

"Listen! Just listen! Merle didn't think he owed it but you know how he is. He gave it to 'em because he thought _____ was sincere about it and he and _____ have always been close and money don't mean that much to him anyway." He puffed one final puff and sadly rubbed the cigarette out.

Hal opened his mouth to say something but Chuck waved him off.

"Let me finish. When I put the facts and figures on Merle and proved it by Steve, they were finished. Screwed. For now and for always. They don't knock anymore of my songs off. They don't knock anymore of your songs off. They are no longer deal killers. Now, I'm swearing you to secrecy because if it ever gets back to either one of 'em, _____ will kill me with Willie. I'll never get another Willie Nelson cut. With one phone call. So, what we've got to do is ——"

The waitress brought the strawberries and Chuck did a funny routine that sent her away laughing. As he mashed up the fruit and milk he said, "You notice I made her forget to add the strawberries to the check. Low budget. Low budget Music Company. Now another thing. You're gonna have to help me with Frances, at B.M.I. Warner Brothers is trying to ruin my career and if she goes along with them, they can do it." He slurped the last of the strawberries and milk. "Damned people have got no sense of humor. Just because I beat them out of sixty grand they want to—"

"Chuck, I can't go and—"

"She believes you. She knows you wouldn't lie to her."

"That's why I can't do it!"

"You can. We both know you can. The question is, will you?" He took the hat off, dropped it on the attaché case, revealing the thinning hair. He leaned across the table and said softly, "Happy," he used the old Fort Worth nickname that only Hal's oldest and closest friends knew about, "You know I've never asked you for help. And Lord knows son, I never was as much help to you as I wanted to be, but—"

"Oh, hell." Hal looked out the window and watched a man and his family climb in to a station wagon. The children were carrying the little Shoney's comic books and had the free suckers in their mouths. He felt exhausted and defeated. He thought of the way a pina colada tasted. "I'm not gonna lie to her."

Chuck seized his hand and squeezed it. "I know that. I don't expect you to. You don't need to. What we do is ——"

The Miracle

He was sleepin' in the yard
up close to the house
When I come out to git the paper
I saw him an went over
an woke him up.

He looked all around,
at first with just his eyes
then he started turnin' his head around
an he said,
"My God! I slep out here in the cold
all night an I'm still alive!"
He sat up then an said,
"I'm not even frozen."
He moved his fingers, openin' an closin'
his fists -
"Not even any frost bite!
It's a miracle!"

I said,
"Oh hell, man, it's the middle of August.
Comon in an git some coffee.
You've probably got a hell of a hangover."

I picked up the paper an he followed
me into the house.
He looked disappointed about losin' his miracle.

Ray Price, 1972

A few days before the Ray Price session, Ray Pennington had called Hal and told him Price had never sent a tape to Cam Mullins. "Cam cain't do the arrangements till he gets that tape. You better take a copy of it out to his house. That's the song he's goin' in to get. He says it's a monster."

Pennington told him how to get to Cam's house and he was driving slowly along the curved street when he saw Cam's wife squatting in the yard, trimming the grass from the sidewalk.

"Cam's in the back of the house working. Just keep banging till he hears you."

Hal rapped on the wood part of the screen door and then turned and watched the woman as she moved in the skin-tight shorts.

The music coming from somewhere inside the house stopped abruptly and in a few moments Cam appeared in the doorway, squinting out into the bright light, a cigarette hanging from his mouth. He came out to take the tape and they stood talking, Cam on the little concrete porch and Hal on the sidewalk. They chatted about the heat and what it was doing to the climber roses, Hal careful not to look at Cam's wife.

"When I do yours, I'll have 'em all. I'm just finishing a Gallico song and I already did 'Oh Lonesome Me.'"

"Gallico song?" Hal felt his stomach muscles suddenly tighten. "Has Gallico finally got to Price?"

Cam flicked the cigarette in an arc that ended in the grass, "Well, you know, it's contract time and things get kind of hairy." He studied Hal's face and then said, "I wouldn't worry about it though, it's a piece of shit. 'She's Got to be a Saint, but I Ain't.' It's a piece of shit. Some New York writers tryin' to write hillbilly. Your tune's the one they're going in to get."

Hal had left the motor running and the air conditioner going. When he leaned back in the seat and put the car in gear, the refrigerated air chilled his sweat-soaked shirt and a shiver went over him.

"Goddamn Gallico!" he thought, feeling the New York publisher's tentacles beginning to wrap themselves around him again. "Even on a Price session there's no way to get a song around the son of a bitch."

He pulled into a driveway across the street and turned back the way he had come, so he wouldn't get lost.

* * *

The night of the session, Hal entered the back door of Columbia Records and walked toward Studio A. Brenton Banks was standing in the hall talking to another string player and he turned to shake hands with Hal, switching a styrofoam cup of coffee to his left hand. "Howzit goin' man? Your tune sounds great."

While he was talking, Hal was reaching around to shake hands with another string player, mumbling greetings and then turning back to Brenton he asked, "He already did it?" wondering about the lyrics.

"Yeah man, it's fine. It's a fine tune."

Brenton was smiling his loving Guru smile, the fringe of hair and the Van Dyke beard white against the indigo skin. He looked straight, and Hal guessed that he hadn't had a chance to go out to the parking lot and smoke pot during the session.

Cynthia came out of the studio, her belly huge under the summer dress. When she saw him, she smiled the happy smile that was always a little tentative, ready to be changed into a wry grin if she was not well received. He saw a quick picture of her as a little girl, mistreated by the grim and embittered mother. The big double violin case she carried dwarfed her and there was something brave and defiant about the tiny pregnant woman that warmed and eased the cold knot in his stomach.

"Where have you been? Have you heard your song? It's great! It came off beautiful! They're going to overdub the Gallico song. It is a piece of shit." She laughed, glancing down the hall to see who was listening.

"Did Price know the song?"

"Did he ever! I'm telling you, it's great. It's a hit." She suddenly became embarrassed at being so exuberant in the presence of the other string players. They were emerging from the studio and hurrying down the hall, clutching their cases and fleeing from the debasement and shame of having been involved with the country music they loathed and mocked, and yet were so dependent upon.

Hal wished they all had to go up to Price and thank him for the money that bought the Mercedes Benz's and the little vases and paintings that, for them, symbolized culture and affluence.

They walked toward the control room, Hal not offering to carry the heavy case, as she told him about the session.

"They got 'Oh Lonesome Me' down right away and then worked on your song for over two hours. Price seemed to be stalling to keep from doing the Gallico song. When they finally finished 'Everything That's Beautiful,' Don Law came out into the studio and talked with Price a minute and then thanked the musicians and told us we could go, but a man in the control room got on the talk back and said, 'The session's not over, we're going to get the last song.' They got it the first take."

"What man are you talkin' about?" Hal paused with his hand on the control room door and turned toward her. "Was it Sherrill?"

"No dummy! Don't you think I know Billy Sherrill?"

"If it wasn't Sherrill, I don't know who it was." He began to feel the knot in his stomach again.

He pushed the door open and let her go past him, the heavy case bumping against his bad knee.

They walked past the little alcove where the sixteen track sat, and he shook hands with Charlie Bradley, the back-up engineer, as the wide tape rewound at high speed.

They continued moving toward the far wall of the control room, past the big black leather couch along the back. There was a love seat and two easy chairs along the side wall where Price's wife and Irene Stanton sat side by side. Hal sat down at the far end of the love seat, in the corner of the room. Cynthia carefully placed the violin case against the seat and then sat down by him, her legs and feet protecting the instruments.

Janie, Price's wife, leaned forward and called past Irene and Cynthia, "Have you heard your song yet?" She was a beautiful brunette, about half Price's age.

Hal leaned forward, "No, we just got here. How'd it come off?"

She clasped her hands in front of her in a gesture of gratitude and said reverently, "It's an absolute monster!"

The knot in Hal's stomach immediately dissolved into warmth and he said, "Great!" and then added with more restraint, "I can't wait to hear it." He hadn't figured her out yet.

Janie introduced Hal and Cynthia to Irene Stanton and told her he had written the ballad.

Irene shook hands with them and said, "Yes, I remember Hal from talking to him on the phone. 'Everything That's Beautiful Reminds Me of You,' what a lovely song!"

"Well thank you, that means a lot coming from a fine songwriter like yourself." He hoped it didn't sound too phony. Irene had used her position as Don Law's secretary-mistress-nurse to become half writer on a lot of songs she had never written any part of. 'Access, my God. In this business it's all access,' he thought, feeling a rush of rebellion again.

Apparently she didn't find anything wrong with his compliment. She gave him a warm smile and said, "I always enjoy your songs." Hal looked around the room. Lou Bradley, Columbia's best engineer was at the board, adjusting the myriad knobs, buttons and switches. He was Charlie and Owen Bradley's cousin. Beyond the console, Price and Cam were standing close together, engrossed in conversation.

Inside the isolation room, Don Law was chatting with Grady Martin, the hulking, morose and aging guitar player, as the other musicians packed their instruments amid the maze of metal chairs, baffle walls and jumbled electric wiring. At the other end of the console stood Cynthia's mystery man, Ron Bledsoe, taut, alert and purposeful.

Bledsoe had big basset hound eyes, but they were hooded and cold, like a pawnbroker's, and he was all business. He was Clive Davis' fair-haired boy sent to Nashville to wrest control from the un-business-like hillbillies and teach them "The Gospel of the Bottom Line."

He made no effort to hide the disdain he felt for the uneducated and disorganized rabble who made the music. To him they were a necessary evil in the otherwise orderly process of getting worthless plastic discs into homes and extracting money to be deposited in New York banks.

He had a Beatle haircut and wore perfectly fitting mod clothes with a medallion hung around his neck on a gold chain, but they were props. Hal had seen him driving his Rolls Royce and thought, 'What a strange sight, a machine driving a machine.'

Clive Davis was the president of Columbia Records and he obviously had a lucrative deal with Al Gallico. Songs from other publishing companies were cut on Columbia sessions but the singles were almost always Gallico songs. In the last year, Hal had gotten a lot of his songs cut by Columbia artists but each time they wound up in the can or on the album and a Gallico song was released as a single. The big money came from the radio performances.

Price was the only one who had refused to play the game. He had never cut a Gallico song and since Don Law produced him independently for Columbia, he was outside the chain of command.

Price turned to the engineer and said, "Play the ballad again, Lou."

Lou turned in the swivel chair and called back to the backup engineer, "Play the ballad, Charlie!"

Charlie stuck his head around the corner, "Is it the first cut or the second one?"

"The second one," Price and Lou said at the same time.

Price came around and sat down in the producer's chair and Cam Mullins walked over and shook hands with Hal. "Have you heard it yet?"

"No, I just got here."

Cam wore a white dress shirt open at the neck and with the cuffs turned back over his forearms. "It's fine, man, fine. One of the best things he's done since 'For the Good Times.'"

Don Law came in from the isolation room and Price got up and turned the chair around to him.

"Sit down Don, they're gonna play the ballad."

Lou had pulled off the white adhesive tape he had used to mark the gain positions for the last song and reset the knobs. He stood up and said, "Sit here Ray, where you'll be in the middle of the speakers."

Price sat down and Charlie's head ducked behind the partition. The tape began to roll.

Cam's voice came over the speakers. "Ah one, ah two, ah one, two, three, four -"

The strings and the steel guitar played the intro and then the familiar baritone began singing,

"Everything that's beautiful reminds me of you,
Everything that spring can bring in shades of green and blue
The sound of children laughing, the rose in morning dew,
Everything that's beautiful reminds me of you."

Price's singing took Hal back to the Texas barrooms and honky tonks of his youth. This was the voice that had woven the dream for a generation of dreamers and losers. They came into the air-conditioned dimness, lit only by the light from the jukeboxes and beer signs, fleeing from the hot dry winds of reality.

"In the first days of my sorrow, I could never realize
Why falling snow or a rainbow would bring teardrops to my eyes
But as lovely scenes brought back lovely dreams, finally I knew,
Everything that's beautiful reminds me of you."

When the tape had first begun to play, Hal had been analyzing the production, examining the mixture of sounds, passing judgment on the instrumentation, but more and more he found himself being drawn into the story of the song. He was thinking of Rita, the girl he had been obsessed with when the song had been written.

Suddenly he realized that this was Price's great talent: that he phrased in a manner that forced the listener to pay attention to the words of the song. He broke the notes down into patterns of human speech so that it was not possible to groove along, listening only to the beauty of the voice and the melody. It was an added dimension of communication. It occurred to him that Price, in order to work all this out and perfect it, would have to be very intelligent.

He looked up and saw Price watching him, his face inscrutable and totally without expression. He knew his own face must have been reflecting the awe and wonder of his discovery and he smiled a warm smile of tribute, but Price's eyes moved to a place on the wall several feet above Hal's head, with no flicker of recognition.

"How can I forget you, or pretend I've never met you
When everything that's pretty always brings you to my mind
In a world so full of beauty every picture is a memory
To forget you I would need to be blind."

As the end of the bridge, the orchestra did a clean modulation and Price began the last verse, which was a repeat of the first verse. Hal felt the goose bumps that always rose up on his arm when he heard something really beautiful.

When the song was over, the electronic entity, which had transported them to another reality, clicked to a stop and turned back into a mass of inert wiring and cooling metal. The people in the control room all came out of wherever they had been and began moving their bodies around, reestablishing contact with the present time and place.

Everyone began to talk at once, the women's excited voices cutting through and overriding the others. Cam was laughing happily, his plastic cup of wine forgotten.

"That's it! That's the one we've been wanting! That's a monster," he said to Price. Price was nodding in grave agreement.

Don Law said, "I think that's definitely the 'A' side single."

Bledsoe moved from the far end of the console like a boxer springs to the middle of the ring when the bell rings. "It's not even a good 'B' side! Play the last song, Lou." His manner was that of a teacher telling the children to get back to work when recess is over.

Don Law's head jerked toward Bledsoe and he stared at him incredulously. Cam froze with his cup halfway to his mouth. Price was the only one whose expression did not change. He seemed detached and deep in thought.

After a quick glance at Don Law, Lou called, "Charlie, play the last song."

They heard Cam counting and then the strings played an intro that was a blurred version of the last four bars of "Home Sweet Home." Price's voice began singing "She's Got To Be A Saint." The knot in Hal's stomach was back and he realized he had stopped breathing as some point. He took a deep breath and slowly ran his hands along the legs of his Levis, attempting to dry the perspiration. As he listened, he realized Cynthia's evaluation of the song was correct. It was a piece of shit.

Bledsoe stood behind Price's chair, listening intently and fingering the gold medallion.

Hal felt an almost overpowering need to stand up, take a half step toward Bledsoe and put all of his weight behind a right hand and see if he could explode the left side of his face. He could see the cheek bone caved in and maybe the left eye hanging out of its socket. They would take him to Vanderbilt and put the eye back in, but they could never restore the cocksure arrogance. For the rest of his life he would be glancing nervously to his left. "He might even become a communist," Hal muttered under his breath.

Cynthia's head spun toward him, "What did you say?"

"Nothing, I've got to go take a leak."

The only restroom he knew about was downstairs and by the time he got back, Price was out in the studio, sitting on a stool in the singer's separation booth.

Lou was back in his chair, Blesoe stood behind him and Don Law sat staring through the half-lensed reading glasses at a notebook, a gold tipped fountain pen in his right hand. Behind the partition, the whir of the sixteen track stopped and Lou said to Don Law, "We're ready, Mr. Law."

The old man's head moved toward the talk-back button, but Bledsoe leaned over and pushed it.

"We're ready in here Ray. Are you ready to put one down?"

Price was adjusting his earphones. If he was surprised at Bledsoe's intervention, his voice betrayed nothing. "Yeah, let's try one."

After the intro, Price began to sing "She's Got to be a Saint." When he had gotten half way through the first verse he stopped, "Lou, can you turn the voice up in the earphones? I can't hear me." The studio was dark except for the control room and the singer's booth.

Lou said, "I've got them up as high as they'll go, Ray. Try another set."

Price took the earphones off, unplugged them and put on another pair. Charlie rewound the tape and they began again.

This time Price got through half of the second verse before he stopped singing.

"Lou, can you turn down the other voice track? I keep hearing the old cut and it's throwing me off."

Lou pushed the engineer's talk back button and said, "Ray, there's not any old track. That's the one we're cuttin' over. It must be bleedin' in from one of the musician's tracks. Lemme see if I can find it." The tape started again and Lou listened to one instrument at a time until he came to the guitar track. You could hear Price singing in the background. "Yeah, that's it. It's Pete Wade's mike. He was up close to the booth and it picked you up. All we can do is pull him down for now, and then bring him in later to overdub his part."

Bledsoe leaned over in front of Law and pushed the button. "Ray, what you had was good, do you want to keep it?"

"Naw, start at the top."

As Price began singing again, Bledsoe kept leaning with his back in Don Law's face until the producer got up and walked over to Irene and asked her to get him a cup of coffee. As soon as he was out of the chair, Bledsoe sat down in it.

As Price sang, and the old Englishman stirred his coffee, Hal reflected on what a really nice man he was. Too nice to tell an artist he was dropping him from the label, too nice to tell an invalid wife he was in love with a rich socialite in Dallas, and too nice to fight with the New York types who were descending on Nashville now that country music was beginning to earn big money.

Hal glanced at Irene and saw her staring at the old man with fierce loyalty. She was the last of a long line of people who had loved him and tried to shield him from the harsh realities that invade an alcoholic's life from time to time.

As Price came in from the studio and passed Bledsoe in order to get to the chair Lou had vacated for him, Bledsoe looked up at him with the smirk that he used for a smile and said, "I think we got it that time!"

Price ignored him and sat down. "How'd it sound, Don?"

The old man looked grateful for the tribute, but the voice came from far away. "Very good, Ray, very good." He took the reading glasses off and dropped them in the pocket of his tweed jacket.

The tape rolled again and as Hal watched Price, he remembered what Clarence Selman had told him on Marigold's boat two weeks before.

"They've got Price over a barrel. His contract is up and he still owes them twenty-seven sides. If he dudn' go along with them, all they have to do is suspend him till he cuts all those sides. And all that time he's suspended, he's still under contract. He can't record for anybody else. And while all that's goin' on, his career's liable to go down the drain. They're holdin' his feet to the fire."

When the tape stopped, Bledsoe stood up, "That's it! It's a smash! I don't hear a thing wrong with it!" Hal saw a little rhythmic spasm in Bledsoe's right eyelid and noticed that his normally pallid face was flushed. Price didn't seem to hear him. He was looking through the wall and off toward the Life & Casualty building, or somewhere.

Bledsoe looked defiantly at Cam.

Cam's little Errol Flynn mustache twitched and he dropped his eyes to study the wine cup in his hand. Doing Price's arrangement had made him the hottest arranger in town, but Columbia was his biggest account.

As everyone watched Price he slowly nodded his head, "Alright." He turned to the engineer, "Lou, on the bridge, I was listening to the other voice when it was bleeding through and I was getting a unison effect. It sounded good. I wonder how it would sound to put me on again, singing in unison on the bridge. Have you got an open track?"

Lou said, "Ray we've got a machine that will delay your voice a fraction of a second and add it at the same time. You won't have to cut it on another track."

Hal nudged Cynthia and stood up.

Janie called, "Are you leaving?"

He stepped over in front of her and put out his hand. "Yeah, we've got a baby sitter that's got to go to school in the mornin'."

She took his hand and pulled him down to whisper in his ear, "I'm sorry about what happened to your song."

"That's alright. I understand. You lose some and you win some."

He shook hands with Price and thanked him for cutting the song, then followed Cynthia out the door.

After he had taken the babysitter home and he and Cynthia were lying in the big four-poster bed, she asked, "How can Price work with a man like Bledsoe? What an awful person!"

"He cain't and he won't. They've won the battle and lost the war. As soon as he cuts the sides he owes them, he'll go to another label." He tried to decide what label he would go to if he were Price.

She yawned and said, "You know I really like Price."

"Yeah, me too. The funny thing about it is, I've been around him a lot of times, over the years, but tonight was the first time I ever really liked him. I guess I wound up understandin' him a little bit."

She reached her hand over and laid it on his chest, "I think you're the greatest songwriter in the world and I sure do love you."

He sighed, "Well, you just have to write so many good songs that they can't screw you out of all of 'em."

After she was asleep, he lay there staring at the ceiling, thinking of all the times this had happened to him since long ago in West Texas when he had begun to write songs.

"Maybe they can screw you out of all of 'em," he thought. "Maybe they can."

Table Manners

Hal was driving down Woodmont Boulevard, talking to Christopher about table manners.

"You know, it's like I keep tellin' you, Christopher, you're not supposed to handle the food in your plate with your left hand. If you need to get somethin' on your fork, you push it on with a piece of bread. That way you don't have to keep wipin' your hand on your britches." They stopped at a red light and Hal looked over at the eight-year-old. He was picking at a loose piece of rubber on his tennis shoe and staring at the dashboard. "Maybe I need to talk to your mother about it so she can help me remind you about it." Hal had been nervous and irritable all day. He had been off the booze for five days. The light changed and they started up again.

Christopher said quietly, "But Dad,— if I act like a grown up all the time—," He turned toward Hal, his face earnest and thoughtful, "people will think I'm a midget!"

Hal broke into laughter. The little boy didn't join in. He was staring at the dashboard again. Hal reached across the seat and squeezed the small thigh.

"Pretty boy, I love you. I'm sorry I get cross with you when I'm nervous."

Christopher looked surprised. "You're never cross with me, Dad."

That was when Hal realized what a mistake he was making trying to require adult behavior of a child.

Home

Sometimes when a storm gathers and slowly builds up, and a sweet smellin' cool breeze moves in ahead of the dark clouds, rufflin' the leaves on the trees and billowin' the curtains, bangin' a door somewhere and then bangin' it again,

a warm soft easy feelin' comes over me an I sit down by the window an watch the storm move in.

I think of you - out in the kitchen, or writin' letters, or payin' bills upstairs, the children asleep in their beds - an some sort of a feelin' of safety surrounds me - and the word "home" comes into my mind.

They say that home is where the heart is, an my heart's belonged to you for a long, long time.

This mornin' when it was rainin' too hard to git outside, an you an me was lookin' at those picture albums Mama sent after Pa passed on, I was tryin' to explain to you how different the world was when I was a kid. The pictures don't really tell it all.

The one with the '54 Chivaley in the driveway, an off to one side, me on my brand new Dixie Flyer bike, an my folks standin' by the car in their Sunday best, cause we'd all jist got home from church, an you can almost hear the sound of katydids in the bright summer sunshine.

Mama's still got her hat on, but there's some flour on the front of her dress an you know she's already been in the kitchen an put the biscuits in the oven an got the chicken to fryin.

My sister's wadn' in the picture. She was probably in her room with the door closed, playin' records by the Platters an dreamin' about love. Probably "Only You," or "Twilight Time," or "Love Me Tender" by that new singer.

In a minute, Mama'd be callin' her to some make a salad an set the table.

A lot of times in the evenin' we'd all sit out on the front porch an I'd be turnin' the crank of the ice cream freezer, makin' peach ice cream, an Pa would start tellin' stories about the way things were when he was growin' up, an we'd sit there in the twilight on the porch an the boy from down the street'd come by on his motor scooter an throw the paper up next to the house, but nobody'd make a move to go get it. Nobody wanted to break the spell. It was like we wanted that time to go on forever.

Then perty soon the streetlights would come on an you could hear parents callin' the names of their kids, an the vacant lot where they'd been knockin' flys with a baseball would empty out an you'd hear the last kid goin' home on his bike, the pedal hittin' the kickstand every time it'd come around, clack, clack, clack.

You know, darlin' sometimes when the children are takin' their naps, or in the middle of a school day, I'll come in an find you in the rockin' chair, rockin' the puppy with your eyes closed an I know you're prayin' an I'll tiptoe on out.

That's when I realize what makes the difference in the way we live, an what's happenin' to most of the world.

I've seen that hand that was strokin' that puppy - rock a cradle, an heal a child's achin' ear, an once or twice wipe the tears from the face of a man who'd almost lost his faith.

Home is where the heart is, an my heart'll always belong to you, now and forever more.

(Hal Bynum, Andite Invasion/BMI From the Albums It's My Time 1995 and If I Could Do Anything 1998)

Apologia

Hal chuckled. Yvonne looked up with interest. He wasn't much of a chuckler and she obviously wondered what it was about.

"I was just thinkin' about the insanity of alcoholism. I used to think I was some kind of a prophet. After I read 'Apologia,' Socrates statement at the time of his death, I began to compare myself to him. I twisted it around in my mind to where I had gone on them drunken rampages, terrorizin' people an tearin' up offices an raisin' hell, well I changed it around to where I had done all that out of some kind of loyalty to the truth, you know, exposing phonies, calling peoples bluffs, whatever. What a bunch of shit!" They had just finished having sex and he was lying naked on the carpet, smoking a Pall Mall and feeling happy, relaxed and expansive.

"I'm not familiar with 'Apologia' so the comparison doesn't enlighten me." Under the smudged makeup her face was beautiful. She was thirty but looked closer to twenty.

He blew out a cloud of smoke and she waved it away. "You wanta hear it?"

"I would say its somewhere between wanting to and bowing to the inevitable."

"You're pretty funny, pretty. A trivial and frivolous little shit, but funny." She laughed happily, "Well Lord knows I try."

"Yeah, well anyway, they were fixin' to kill 'im. Socrates, I mean."

"Who else?"

"They asked him if he had anything to say and he says, 'Well I know there must be a bunch of you here today that's puzzled about all of this, especially if you happen to be from out of town. There's probably some of you that might want to ask, 'Socrates, how'd you manage to git yourself in such a fix?' It might occur to you that there's somethin' unusual about me cause it's not that often that the whole town of Athens gits together and decides to kill somebody. 'How'd you go about distinguishin' yourself like that?'"

Yvonne was laughing, "Are you sure he wasn't from Amarillo?"

"No, it's the translation."

"I believe it."

"Anyway he says, 'I'll try to explain it the best I can. What happened was, this friend of mine, he was kind of a jake-legged, half-assed, shade-tree philosopher,'" Hal paused — "(I guess he couldn't have been a philosopher, since this all happened before Philo was born) an he went to the oracle of Delphi an he ast her, 'Oracle, whose the smartest man in the world?' and she says, 'Why Socrates of Athens, who else?' An this here friend comes back an tells me about it an I thinks, 'Well looky here, I've finally got that broad dead to rights,' cause I knew that not only was I not the wisest man in Athens, I wadn' ebm' wise at all. I knew all I had to do was go out an find a man wiser'n me an her ass would be shinin' like new money. So I proceeds to go an look up this feller I'd been thinkin' was wise for years, an I sidles up to 'im and commences to listen.

'He's got a big crowd of his followers an hangers on an snuff queens around 'im, an I commenced to listening to what he was sayin' an before long it come to me that he was as full of shit as a Christmas goose,'"

Yvonne interrupted, "This was before Christmas too."

"An so anyway, he says 'Since I wadn' wise and I knew I wadn', and this feller wadn't wise and didn't know it, I figured that put me ahead of him, an I knew I had to go look somewhere else. But before I left, out of loyalty to the Truth, I got up an exposed his ignorance to his group an his groupies. An of course he hated me for it, an his group hated me, 'cause I took away what they'd been leanin on, an — well I jist went all over town doin' that an - that's how come you see me here today, in the fix I'm in.'"

Yvonne wasn't laughing anymore. "That's what all the prophets did, wasn't it?"

Hal put the cigarette out. "Yeah, more or less."

We Had It All Figgered Out

We had it all figgered out,
logo and all
we talked allot about next year
nobody said a word about the long haul
at last the big, big, big one
was gonna fall in our lap
the world would beat a path to our door
We had a better mouse
we had a better trap
we had it all figgered out

Don't you love the way we looked?
All them stars in our eyes?
No room for gloom
total strangers to sad surprise

We took allot of pictures
guaranteed to please
here's some we took later
Let's don't look at these
the light's not right
I don't quite like the poses
everthaing definitely wasn't comin' up roses

In this one we look a little tired
must have been late in the day
We'd begun to lose a little bit of force
but they told us it was only natural
and more or less par for the course

Hangin' on through the bad times
that's what it's all about
we didn't doubt it for a minute
We had it all figgered out.

Here's a picture of us and Aunt Sally
we're all smilin', holdin' up the check
Our very first investor
(wonder who we're gonna hit on next?)

Here's a snapshot somebody
made of us movin'
I'm grinnin' at the camera and clownin'
looks like I'd had a few beers
I can tell by your face it musta
been rainin' -
Surely to God it wadn't tears

Here's one of me sorta smilin'
by an older model car
sometimes you gotta do some downsizin'
if you really wanta be a star

Here's one Uncle Mort made of Aunt Sally
knockin' on our door
We musta neglected to tell 'er
we didn't live there no more

All in all it's a really great
picture album
In the last ones you could
see a little doubt

I like the first pictures better
when we had it all figgered out.

I Wanta Be

I wanta be a cool drink of water
That quenches the thirst of a man
Who works in a field that yields
The golden grain

I wanta be the ointment
That the mother gently rubs on the child
And after awhile it eases the pain

I wanta be the memory in the mind
Of a woman who's gone blind
And bring back beautiful scenes from her youth

I wanta be the plant that grows the cotton
The fact that's not forgotten
I wanta be the moment when the innocent man
Is saved by the Truth

I wanta be the knife that cuts the bullet
From the soldier's arm
The chunk of coal that keep the children warm

I don't ask to be the whole machine
Just one of its tiny moving parts
Just one note of the symphony
That reaches all ears and opens all hearts

I wanta be the rainbow that signals the end of bad weather
I wanta be the gray of the dawn
When the long night of anger is gone
I wanta be one word in a message of hope
That brings all of mankind together

I wanta be the quiet voice in the ear
Of the condemned man who's filled with fear
As he stands on the gallows, and his lips begin to quiver,
I wanta tell him there's a new life waiting
On the other side of the river

I wanta be the love in the eyes of a young mother
As tiny fingers grip her hand
I wanta be the wind of forgiveness

That sweeps across the land
I wanta be the message of mercy that makes all men free

I WANTA BE, I WANTA BE, I WANTA BE.

(Hal Bynum Andite Invasion/BMI From the Album If I Could Do Anything 1998)

Sugar

Hal's mother, who always took care of him and was always on his side, always remembering he was a little child who still had almost everything to learn, and who constantly endeavored to protect him and his older sister from the seething, cornered-rat rage of their father, forgot, on that particular night, to make sure the little boy emptied his bladder before he went to bed.

Hal slept between his parents in the white painted iron bed stead in the two-story wooden farm house which shook and sagged under the weight of the icy arctic winds that swept down from Canada, howling across the frozen and barren crust of the great plains, hurling itself against the fragile, man-made obstruction, moaning and subsiding and then suddenly renewing the assault with a new level of intensity.

Sometime late in the night, Hal was dreaming and in the dream he needed to urinate and he was unable to find a place to relieve himself and the painful pressure in his bladder was unbearable. In the vague environs of the dream, he finally found a place and with great gratitude and a long satisfied sigh, he released the fluid, relaxing and drifting deeper into sleep and peace.

Suddenly a loud roar assaulted his slumber and a giant force grasped his arm, pinning him, face down, to the wet sheet as a series of explosions were rained down on his back and bottom. His flesh was on fire as he screamed out, his child's voice joining the sound of the roaring, which, he half realized, was his father's voice shouting at him behind and above the meat on meat impact sound of the descending blows.

He heard his mother's voice crying, "Tommy! Tommy! That's enough!"

Finally, it was over and the numbing hold on his arm was loosened and Hal immediately and instinctively turned over, face up to protect his back which was on fire. Through tears, he observed his father, on his knees in the bed, holding his wet undershirt out from his chest, his contorted face, dark red and his eyes shining crazily, his voice unrecognizable in its animal rage.

Hal was older than his father had been at the time of the beating before he realized that the reason he could see all of the scene the way he could still see it, was because the kerosene lamp was burning. His father had found a match and lit the lamp so he could see what he was doing. The act was deliberate.

The next day the little boy was playing quietly with some wooden blocks near the coal stove when the man came in through the front door of the house. Hal bent down further over the toys. He had heard the tractor stop in the front yard and a bolt of fear had gone through his body and his back had begun to burn again.

He heard the footsteps as they approached and saw the man's feet in front of him. He didn't look up as the voice began to berate him again, picking up where it had left off the night before. Hal began to shake and to swallow and choke back the sobs that were shaking his insides. If you cried you got another whipping. That was the way it worked.

Then, his mother's hand was on his right arm, lifting him, gently, but firmly from the linoleum covered floor, guiding him toward the front door, her voice pleading with the angry man as she put the little coat on the boy and placed a piece of candy in his hand.

Then he was outside, listening to the strident voices as they reached through the wood and glass, clearly discernable in the cold morning stillness. Last night's wind was gone and the dark, bare limbs of the trees stood silent and still.

Hal walked out to one of the old locust trees, circled around it and sat down on the ground, putting the tree between himself and the voices. He looked down and saw the stick of candy in his right hand and slowly brought it to his mouth, staring out across the endless, openness of the West Texas winter. The sugar began to dissolve in his wet mouth and a warmness crept through his body. He leaned back against the tree and closed his eyes. He sucked at the candy stick, twirling it slowly in his mouth and the warmth and feeling of well being increased as he began to fantasize about being big and strong and safe.

For most of his life, Love and understanding would elude Hal, but sugar had become the warming and soothing friend who was nearly always available, and he was able to use it to escape from a world which was sadly lacking in Love. It, along with his fertile and creative imagination, transported him to a world where things were like he wanted them to be. He knew nothing of addiction or how it isolated its devotees, creating temporary options to reality, preoccupying one with self, with one's immediate comfort, with taking, rather than giving, with the loneliness of self-absorption.

If he has known all of it, he would have still done as he did.

Someone had once said, "There are many people who, only after great tribulation, may enter the kingdom."

Hal was one of those people.

It was alright.

Eventide

His mom caught him napping with his spoon in his hand
and she picked him up from his high chair,
"It's time for bed little man."
He tried to escape her, he started to rebel
he thought about kicking and started to yell

But his chocolate chip anger and Post Toasty venom
couldn't support violence, he didn't have it in 'im
Besides, he was too tired for a tantrum
his weary eyes were blinded by the light
So he waved weakly to the grownups
and said a sad, soft
"Night, night."

Trying To Lose Weight

Tryin' to lose weight, tryin' to lose weight
Ten more pounds and I'll look great
But all I do is procrastinate - and eat

I went walkin' just to burn up calories
Joggin' real fast past museums and art galleries
But when I got to the market place
My saliva started to flow
I came to a full stop and poked my head inside a butcher shop
Cause I swear to God
I thought I heard a pork chop say hello

Tryin' to lose weight, tryin' to lose weight
I been tryin' to calculate
When I'll get stuck in my front gate
I'm tryin' to lose weight

Duck, beef, ham and chicken
Goose and quail, they're all finger lickin'

I finally lost a pound, so to celebrate
I took a pretty girl on a dinner date
The home cooked food was the finest in the south
She watched me eat a whole roast pig and the apple in its mouth
Now when I call, she's always out

Cheese and grits, greens and poultry
Homemade bread - that's all good groceries

I gotta friend that's a wholesale grocer from outta state
He can get me barrels of pickled pigs feet
And double yoked eggs by the crate

Tryin' to lose weight, tryin' to lose weight
I used to be a fashion plate
Now I can't breath in a size forty-eight

Beans and corn, veal and mutton
I love it all - Lord I'm a glutton

I put some sugar free cookies by my bed on a plate
But they was so dry, I had to wash 'em down with a ribeye steak

Me and Will Rogers was a whole lot alike
I never met a chocolate pie that I didn't like
Tryin' to lose weight, tryin' to lose weight.....

(Hal Bynum, Andite Invasion/BMI From the Album The Promise 2002)

"Chains, Chains, Shackles and Chains"

Tex Whitson, Merle Haggard's manager at the time, turned back around and faced Hal in the booth. He had been twisted around, staring at the other end of the restaurant, waiting for Hal to finish the plate of pancakes. He reached out his right hand and slowly turned the metal syrup container with his forefinger, then turned it back, his half-closed eyes studying the movement.

"What's Tony Brown got against you?"

Hal's hand slowed down as he lifted a fork-load of hash brown potatoes toward his mouth, but it didn't stop. He appeared to ignore the assault, waiting to see what came next.

Tex's style of doing business was adversarial and pugnacious. He came at you like Jake Lamotta, leaning into you, his head on your chest, hooking with both hands, bobbing and weaving, crowding and punishing, trying to force an opening.

Hal laid the fork on the plate, pushed it back a couple of inches with his thumbs, and reached into his left shirt pocket with his right hand, digging out a cigarette from the pack. Tex's hooded eyes darted to the pocket and instantly back to the metal syrup pitcher. He hated to have to smell smoke. He had quit years before.

Hal tore the filter off the cigarette, lit it and blew a huge ball of smoke down onto the top of the table where it would rise up into Tex's face. You had to fight Tex the way Robinson fought Lamotta, keep the left jab in his face, glide back out of the way when he charged in and wait for the chance to throw the left hook and right cross. Tex was tough and devious. He had a grim and sardonic wryness, which masqueraded as humor, and a plodding tenacity that was tireless.

"Tony Brown at M.C.A.?" Hal said it as though the name were vaguely familiar.

Tex's forefinger continued to turn the pitcher. "Yeah, Tony Brown at M.C.A."

"The Tony Brown Bowen hired and gave him his big break and now he talks against Bowen behind his back? That Tony Brown?"

Tex's face turned a light purple, starting at his neck and moving up into the salt and pepper grey of his brush cut hair. Hal smiled inwardly as he heard the anger in the heavy-set man's voice.

"The Tony Brown who produces country music records that sell in stores and make money!" He finally lifted his eyes to glance at Hal, "You do make your livin' writin' songs or are you still rich off 'Lucille' and semi-retired?" He pushed the syrup can away, darted his hand to the back of his head and worked the back of his neck as though it were sore. He glanced around the restaurant and then looked at Hal with boredom on his face and in his voice. "You might want to send Christopher to college one of these days, you reckon maybe?"

Hal shook his head, his mouth full of coffee, "Readin' books clouds the brain. Imona teach 'im to hang dry wall. Work inside when the weather's bad. Like today." He turned his head and stared through the window at the gray and wet Nashville street. 'Wintertime, Music City,' Hal thought, 'I need to be in Miami Beach.'

"The reason I asked you about him was I was talkin' to the security guard that works at the back door of C.B.S. yesterday an he said evertime he sees Tony in the parking lot, he hollers an asks him. 'When you gonna release Chains?' an Tony turns white in the face an hollars back, 'NEVER! That's when!'"

Hal turned from the window. It was starting to snow. He took another drag from the cigarette and this time he blew the smoke away from Tex. He liked the man a lot, he just got tired of the way he crowded in all the time.

Tex saw he was listening now and he softened his tone. "People all over town are kiddin' him about it. One of my friends over at CBS called him up the other day and said, 'When you gonna release Hal Bynum's song? You know it's a hit!' Tony said, 'I don't give a damn!' an slammed the phone down." An honest amazement had crept into Tex's tone, "What in the world did you do to the little jerk, throw him out of a window?"

"I never did nothin' to 'im. I barely know 'im." Hal had decided to keep quiet about it. If it got around, it would make it worse.

As the temperature dropped outside, someone kept turning the heat higher inside and Hal took off the brown Stetson, crushed and brim-rolled like a rancher's hat, and laid it on the seat beside him. He unbuttoned the cuffs on his custom-tailored, vaguely western cut, pale blue shirt and rolled the sleeves up two turns.

"He swears he's not gonna release it." Tex said, watching Hal carefully.

"He'll have to if the jocks pull it out of the album. That's what happened before, you know." Hal was watching Tex through the top of his glasses as he slowly butted out the cigarette in the little glass ashtray.

Tex through his head back and laughed, "Man, you throw 'Lucille' around like it was World War II!"

Hal laughed with him. "Butler didn't want to put that one out either. The jocks forced it out."

Tex turned and slid his feet out into the aisle as though he were about to leave, but instead he sat staring down at his lizard-skin boots, cocking his head back and forth, studying them intently.

Hal said, "You know George wanted to cut 'Chains,' but when Sherrill called and asked Tony what he was gonna do with it, he told him it was Patty's next single, but then it wadn't." Tex had turned his head and was watching Hal again. "Yeah, Mark, over at Lorimar told me when Tony lied to him twice, telling him it was gonna be a single and then it wadn't, he sent a tape to Jones. He said Nancy called him an begged him to hold the song for George. Said he had played it over and over ever since they got it. He thought it was the best thing he'd heard in years."

Tex nodded, looking down at the boots again, "He don't want to put it out, but he don't want nobody else to have a hit on it."

Hal sighed and extracted another cigarette from his shirt pocket, "Several acts have wanted to cut it, but he tells them it's the next single and they're afraid to cut it. By the time they find out he's lyin' they've already cut somethin' else an put it out." He lit the Merit 100 after he had pulled off the filter and dropped it in the ashtray. Tex was nodding in agreement. "Highway 101; Tony's done it to Paul Worley three times. Worley swears he's gonna cut it anyway, no matter what Tony does. Ta hell with it. Cut it an come with it!"

The big gray haired man stood up, put on his jacket and retrieved his brief case from the booth. "I've gotta go hit a lick. I'm not independently wealthy." He grabbed the check before Hal could get it. "Maybe you ought to go over an talk to Tony. Find out what he's got against you. It's gotta be somethin' strong to turn down a hit record outta spite."

Hal watched him walk swiftly to the cash register, pulling his billfold from the hip pocket of his western cut dress pants. Hal tried to catch the waitress' eye, holding his coffee cup high.

After she came and filled his cup and cleared away the dishes and food remnants, Hal sat in the booth, sipping coffee and smoking cigarettes, reexamining the strange situation that had developed around the song, "Chains." He knew why the producer hated him, and there was nothing he could do about it. Hal was not the villain in the story, for once. If he had been, he might have gone to the young producer and made some sort of apology and straightened it out. Hal had, without meaning to, or understanding what was going on, helped Tony see a part of himself that he was ashamed of, enabled him to discover a facet of his inner being that he was ashamed of, and he hated Hal for it.

When the waitress saw he was not going to leave, she brought a plastic container of coffee and left it. He refilled his cup, lit another cigarette and gazed around the room, looking at people without seeing them.

Several years earlier, when Jimmy Bowen had hired Tony Brown to produce some acts at M.C.A., someone had told Hal that Tony was going to record a new girl singer and he was interested in "One More Last Chance," another song Bud Reneau and Hal had written. Hal had called Tony and he had asked Hal to bring him a tape of the song, plus any other things he had that were somewhat pop flavored and would fit a female vocalist. He had heard Bruce Channel's old record of it somewhere. Probably Bowen had played it for him.

Hal put several songs on a tape and took them to M.C.A. which at that time, was in a concrete building on the corner of 17th and West End Avenue. It was on top of a parking lot and Hal took the elevator up to the third floor and a receptionist called Tony.

He came out immediately, waving Hal toward his office, a little dark bearded man wearing droopy old style clothes from the sixties, apparently some new wave thing from the west coast. Hal had seen John Hyatt wearing a get-up just like it. He decided it had something to do with "Miami Vice."

When they got into the office, Hal saw it was full of promotion and sales people and they were all laughing and guffawing, watching something on a television set.

Tony called, "Run it back to the first. I want Hal to see this." He motioned Hal into a chair in front of the set, as a young man wearing a baseball cap rewound the video, chatting and joking with four or five more record promo types sitting and lounging on desks and chairs, all of them facing the T.V. and V.C.R.

Hal sat in his starched wrangler jeans, his tan cow hide boots and his tapered, subtly western cut shirt with a tall collar, his hat in his lap, politely waiting to watch whatever they wanted him to see, ready to appreciate and make positive comments, fitting in, being likable and affable, playing a role that was new and difficult for him. 'Just sit here and be a phony son of a bitch. There's money involved.'

Hal had expected some country act or some comedy act, but when the video started, he saw that it was a homemade job: somebody carrying a cam-corder. It looked like Florida, or maybe bayou country in Louisiana; somewhere where everything was green and there was a lake or the Gulf in the background.

An affable, smiling, friendly used car salesman type was interviewing people, playing to the camera, making fun of a series of youngsters who, Hal soon realized, were severely retarded. Their eyes went off in different directions, their mouths hung open and their speech was barely intelligible, as they strained and grunted and tried to respond to the interviewer's questions. He spoke to them in a kindly tone, but the content of his questions and comments was derisive and invariably set them up to answer in a way that made them ridiculous.

Everyone but Hal was roaring with laughter, hollering at each other and pointing toward the confused and disoriented misfits, straining to cooperate with the man who was asking questions, their eyes bugging out and their lips fluttering, their faces contorted as they attempted to form words and put together sentences. As they talked, they would pick violently at their clothes or wring their hands, twisting their bodies, their eyes sometimes rolling upward as though they were looking to heaven for answers and assistance.

As the screams of laughter and the shouting and staggering around filled the room with chaos, Hal glanced to his right where Tony was leaning back against a desk, watching Hal intently, a smile beginning to die from his lips. Hal suddenly realized that he had an expression of horror, anger and disgust on his face and as he turned back to observe the hooting and screaming that was going on around the T.V., he forced his face to relax and be, he hoped, unreadable.

His trouble was the anger that threatened to lurch out of control. He could barely get his breath. He had an almost overpowering urge to pick up a wooden chair that was to his left and within his reach and bring it down with all his strength into the face of the man with the baseball cap who was capering about hollering, "My God! My God!"

They were all helpless with laughter and he figured he could cripple or seriously injure all of them before people ran in from other rooms to stop him. His whole body tensed and straining, he came within a hair's breadth of seizing the chair and hurling himself toward them. He fought loose from the terrible impulse, but the struggle to keep from doing it left him weak and shaking, and his head turned toward Tony. He saw the producer staring at him; his eyes were slits of burning anger, his jaw tight, a look of offence and betrayal on his face.

Hal stood up, walked out the open door of the room, heading for the stairway, not willing to wait for the elevator.

* * *

Outside the pancake house, snow had covered the parking lot and all the cars parked there. The building across the street that had once housed Ireland's Restaurant was almost invisible as the huge flakes filled the air. Hal decided to smoke one more cigarette before he left.

Even if he were willing to tell the story, he knew no one would believe it. That Tony Brown had refrained from recording, "One More Last Chance" with the pop flavored girl singer, they would believe. They would believe it because everybody in town knew what a large part ego played in the record business. They would believe that several years later, when someone pitched "Chains" to Tony and his new girl singer, Patty Loveless, that he would devise the scheme of cutting Hal's song and burying it in an album, keeping other artists from cutting it by telling them it was Patty's next single, because that was an old Billy Sherrill trick devised years ago. If someone brought you an obvious hit, you knew if you didn't cut it, somebody across the street would, and you'd be fighting it in the charts. Sherrill figured it was just good business. Cut it and not release it, keep promising to release it next.

What they wouldn't believe was that even after disc jockeys were demanding it be released as a single and everybody in town was telling Tony he had a monster hit, that he would refuse that kind of success, for himself, for his artist and for the record label. That was what was hard to believe.

As Hal pulled on his sheep-lined coat and put on his hat, he was amazed that he had never run into Tony when he was drunk and roaming around town at night looking for fights. He didn't figure he would have stomped him, because he was a little guy, but it would have been nice to back-hand him a time or two.

Doodads and Trinkets

She was my wife's old maid aunt
and she was forgetful and wistful and strange.
She lived in a room over the garage
with a one eyed yellow tabby cat
and an old Yorkshire terrier
that was eat up with the mange.
She had always gone and seen after the sick
and set up all night with folks when theyuz dyin'.
She knew everbody from Johnson City to White's Crick
an families always let her take some little what not
that had belonged to the ones who hadn't made it.
Her room looked like a brick o' brack graveyard.
She kept the blinds drawed on one side of the bedroom:
somebody had give her a fire-engine red bedspread
and she didn't want the afternoon sun to fade it.

She wrote a novel about a bunch of people
that got killed by volcanoes on a South Sea island,
but she never sent it off because she couldn't
figure out whether to name it
"Doomed Island of the Damned"
or "Damned Island of the Doomed."
She kept it locked in an old cedar chest in her room.
When she got real old, she wouldn't cook.
People claimed it was cause she lost her gumption,
but it was cause she was never hungry.
That's the way you get when you've got consumption.

I guess it was me that accidentally caused her death:
she called me up to see her and she could barely get her breath.
She asked me if I'd bring a can of paint and brighten up her room.
She died of gallopin' pneumonia, the doctor said it was from the fumes
We left her room the way it was and I went
up there the other day and saw all them little dolls and
whatnots sittin' everwhere on tables and dressers and shelves,
gettin' dustier and the designs gettin' fainter,
and a lot of em had specks and spots of white on em
- cause I've always been a sloppy painter.

"Bud"

Bud had recently had "call waiting" added to his phone service and on this Saturday afternoon, he had his girlfriend, Annette, on one line, his side kick, Buddy, on the other and was, from time to time, kibitzing with his wife, Elke, who was watching a fashion show on television and laughing about the clothes and the models. His German police dog, Rommel, was barking and whining and pawing at the half-glass door that led to the back yard, but they were used to it, and neither of them was conscious of the noise.

Bud had his head cocked to the right and his right hand held the receiver, his fingers cupped around the mouthpiece so as to muffle his soft, whispering voice and make his words unintelligible to Elke. From time to time, the pretty blond woman's laughter would peal out and she would call, "George, would you look at that! That thing is so tight she can hardly walk!"

Bud was watching the T.V. as he talked and he would say something appropriate before returning to the soft, quiet, mumble-whisper-murmur he fed into the phone. He was trying to reason with Annette. She had made up her mind to take a job at the "Classic Cat" nightclub as a topless dancer. Every time he thought of her performing for a bunch of drunks, semi-nude and hanging around the joint, drinking and flirting with customers, he felt a sinking feeling in his stomach and he had to fight off an onslaught of burning rage.

She was nineteen years old, had two children by two different husbands, a father who was a multi-millionaire with whom she was engaged in an unending emotional and financial struggle and had a half-a-lid-a-day marijuana habit.

On this late Saturday afternoon, he was arguing with Annette over his Valium prescription on one line, and switching back and forth to try and talk Buddy into letting Annette and her two children move into the house he shared with his girlfriend and a Labrador retriever named Rocky. Annette's dad had just cut her off, "without a cent" to try and force her to go back to school. Neither of her husbands would pay child support and one of them, a drunken bartender, was stalking her and threatening to kill her.

Bud felt an overpowering need to protect her, to nurture her and to shield her from an unkind world, to hold her, to comfort her and to breathe in the beauty and the innocence, the true, childlike innocence, which was her real nature. He wanted to save her from herself. He wanted to save her from the dangerous immaturity which was always ready to cast aside safety and even reality itself, when the lure of momentary pleasure, the sparkle of promised excitement caught her eye. He wanted to be her protector, but she was so "flaky," so whimsical, so incautious in her habits and in her inclinations, that his lectures and admonitions had no effect. She was a laughing, lovable, charming child, incapable of restraint and unamenable to anything that even remotely approached self-discipline. She was addicted to the glamour of unreality, with all its tawdry trimmings.

Bud believed that the only thing she viewed realistically was himself. For some reason, he was unable to explain, she saw him as he really was, somehow grasping that he was not like other people saw him, a failure because of his inability to conform to society, but rather a genius who would "show them all someday." She knew that his unwillingness to be ground under the foot of big business; allowing his individuality to be destroyed by attempting to operate by rules someone else had made up, was all that had kept him from being "famous already."

Bud was amazed that she could understand him so deeply and so quickly. They were in complete accord as to the inevitability and immanence of his success, notwithstanding how bad things looked at present.

They sat for hours in his Volkswagen rabbit, late at night, smoking dope and planning how it would all be when he hit. He would, of course, take care of Elke and the girls financially, making sure they had everything they needed, and Annette would be free at last from having to "hassle with Harley and Robert over child support," and the necessity for "begging my dad like a dog for a few lousy dollars and kissing his drunk-alcoholic-rich-bitch young wife's ass just to be able to pay my bills!" They could fly to the Bahamas, and to L.A. for Bud to pick up his pop awards, and "smoke killer dope every day and drink the best wines and let 'em all go screw themselves!"

As they sat on a hill above Bellevue, looking down at the lights below, she waved the burning joint grandly, wasting the precious smoke he still owed for. She said, "Bud, don't you see, it's all there for us. You don't have to buckle under to those bastards! I heard that damn Hal tell you the other day that you could have been a millionaire if you would have just shown up on time and been dependable!" She shrieked with laughter, "Oh, wow, him talking to you about being dependable and he was so drunk he couldn't stand up!" She handed him what was left of the joint and turned sideways in the seat, facing him. "Oh, Bud, you're so good. Nobody understands you the way I do." She gripped his forearm as he sucked at the reefer, "I've seen tears in your eyes when you talked about your girls not having lunch money. You care! I don't know anybody that cares like you do!"

She glared angrily at the city beyond the windshield, "To hell with those goddamn bastards! To hell with how much money you owe! Darlin' you're a genius! You've got more talent in your little finger that Hal's got in his whole damn bald-headed body! You don't have to show up on time just because some bastard says that's the time to show up! You're gonna make it so big they'll —. Darlin', can we go get a six pack? I've got some money in my purse."

Bud was reliving the conversation as he waited for her to call back, listening to Elke criticize the stylish clothes on the T.V. show. He wasn't seeing the gaunt girls parading the strange looking dresses. He was seeing the golden haired, beach bronzed, taut butted, lovely who had the most beautiful smile he had ever seen. She was the best since Kristin, he thought, a little touch of sadness sliding in from the past.

Elke laughed, "George would you look as the way that thing hangs on her? I don't think it's even her size!"

* * *

Bud drove past the B.P. station where he knew he could have replaced the worn fan belt. He could hear a loose piece thumping softly under the hood and knew that before long, it would break, but he didn't want to stop and fool with it. It had been that way several days. It was probably good for another day or two.

A hit song would solve everything. His mind flew to the Patty Loveless cut of "Chains." That would do it. The whole town knew it was a hit and it sat there, a winner for everyone who was involved, waiting to burst forth from every radio station in the nation, turning the wheel that made the money, opening the door to more cuts, more success, more recognition. And it sat there, unexploited, unrealized because of Tony Brown's hatred for Hal.

As Bud stopped at a red light, he leaned over and looked in the rear view mirror, fluffing his hair and examining his mustache. He had left the dye on a little too long and gotten it too dark. Everyone but Annette had kidded him about it. A honk came from the car behind him and Bud leaned back to the steering wheel, starting the car to rolling again, hearing the fan belt thumping and wondering if there was anything he could do to get the record released. He couldn't think of anything. If Bowen were still at M.C.A...., but he wasn't. He had moved to Capitol and Bruce Hinton, a pop music man from the West Coast, was running M.C.A.

The whole town was talking about the strange situation and Bud was afraid the story would be told to Hal and Hal would go over to M.C.A. when he was drunk, pull Tony out in the street and cuff him around or worse. If Hal were drunk enough or angry enough, he might not care that Tony was a little short fellow.

He steered with his left hand as he bounced and leaned for a quick view of the mustache. It was awfully dark. He tried to remember how many times they had been blocked because of some senseless enmity Hal had caused during his drunken carousing. It was unbelievable, incredible, that a person with Hal's talent and opportunities would choose to live a life that was totally self-destructive. He thought of what it would do to Christopher when Hal got killed; it was certain to happen, sooner or later.

Bud had saved Hal several times in situations where guns and knives were involved, where Hal was assaulting one person and another came at him from outside the limits of his vision. Bud never involved himself unless someone pulled a weapon. Hal was the reason a number of men armed themselves when they went to music row nightspots and kept guns in their offices. It was only a matter of time till someone killed him.

Bud remembered the crazy man with the steel plate in his head who had jumped Hal three times with a knife coming out of the darkness where he would lurk around the places Hal frequented. Each time Hal had managed to take the knife away from him, but had then refused to beat him up because he felt sorry for him.

The law of averages would catch up with Hal, and Christopher and all the people who, inexplicably, still loved the charming, funny, tortured songwriter, would be saddened, but not surprised. Bud tried to determine how it would effect his own career when it happened. Would people cut Hal's songs once he was dead? Bud and Hal had a large catalogue of really good songs they had written together. He believed the songs they had co-written represented the best of Hal's work and when they were recorded by the right singers, they would realize the same kind and degree of success Hal had had with "Lucille" and his other hits.

Bud believed the best songs he, himself, had written were the songs he had written with Dobie Gray. He fondled a mental list of them as he drove. They were beautiful pop songs and pop-flavored country songs, all of them with a commercial groove, all of them the tried and true, workable, sure fire expressions that had always made money and created career excitement in the music business.

He was driving leisurely through a section of Old Hickory Boulevard which was as yet unpopulated, consisting of unbroken expanses of oak, tulip poplar and hackberry trees, a winding stretch of highway he always enjoyed. He was in no hurry. He liked to arrive late so people would be keyed up and expectant. He liked for Annette to swarm all over him when he finally appeared at her door.

He leaned over and peered into the little rear-view mirror, straining to see his image in the dim light, fluffing his hair again.

Fathers and Sons

When my son, Christopher, was about nine years old, I was still smokin' cigarettes an he wanted to be like me an wear stuff like I wore an he wanted to smoke cigarettes.

Course, I told him he couldn't and why an....I didn't thaink anymore about it until one day they called me from a super market an told me he an another little boy had been caught tryin' to steal a package of cigarettes.

When I entered the room where the security guard was keeping the little boys, my eyes went straight to Christopher. He was holdin' his head up an he wadn't cryin', but I'll never forget the look of shame on his face as his eyes met mine.

I dropped the other little boy off at his house, an on the way home I glanced over at Christopher. He was lookin' straight ahead at the dashboard. Finally, I broke the silence, "Son, I want you to remember how you feel right now. All your life you're gonna do thaings that make you feel good about yourself an from time to time, you're gonna do thaings that make you feel bad about yourself. You're the only one that can make those choices."

I stopped at a red light an while we were sittin' there I said, "You've always been a wonderful boy, all your life. It's been hard on you that your mother an me are divorced, an it's hard for you to understand, but I thaink you've handled it awful well - better'n either one of us has. You've always been good-hearted an unselfish an you're a hard tryer."

The light changed an I drove on down the street. I looked over at him. His little blond head was bent over an he was pickin' at a piece of rubber on his tennis shoe.

"Since I don't git to see you except on weekends, I don't tell you what to do and try to run your life. For one thaing, you've always been smarter'n me, an level-headed. You always see the main thaing an that's a great gift, believe me.

"But, I want to tell you this - whatever kinda trouble you git into - whatever you might have done that you're ashamed of, however embarrassed you are about it, you can always come to me an talk to me... an I won't git mad, or look down on you, or jump in an take over an tell you what you have to do, or go tell somebody else or - any of that. I'll just listen an, if I can, help you figger it out. An - if I do give you some advice - you won't have to take it."

I pulled into the driveway behind my house an before we got out of the car I said, "The thaing is, a young boy might - well - sometimes you might not want to get help cause you thaink you've done sumpm awful an - it probably won't be that bigga deal - but that's a lonely place to be - not knowin' what to do, an bein' afraid to ask somebody. What I'm sayin' is, youc'n talk to me about it. I been in some messes at times an I know what it's like. So you could talk to me an it wouldn't change my opinion of you, or I wouldn't make some big, long speech about it, I'd jist listen and help you it I could - an if you wanted me to.

"I'm on your side, whatever happens. I thaink you're wonderful."

We started to git outta the car, an he stopped with his door half-way open an said, "Dad, are you gonna tell Mom about this?"

I thought about it a little bit and then I said, "No, I'm not gonna teller. But you might wanta teller. She's on your side too."

As we were walkin' into the house he said, "I'll tell her about it."

I reached out and towseled his head and said, "You're a good boy, son. A really good boy."

(Hal Bynum, Andite Invasion/BMI From the Album The Promise 2002)

The Change, (A Kind of a Christmas Carol)

Tonight the whole house smells like cakes and pies, and downstairs I hear the kids decoratin' the Christmas tree. Somewhere in the house a radio's playin' "O Little Town Of Bethlehem."

I've been sittin' here staring through the fallin' snow at a gas light in our front yard. I keep thinkin' about a Christmas Eve when I was a boy. It was snowin' then too, an my mother was downstairs bakin' the same stuff my wife's bakin' now. My grandmother was tuckin' me into bed an talkin' to me, and my Dad was standin' in the door waitin' to turn off the light by my bed. He was ashamed of me bein' scared of the dark.

Before he came upstairs, I'd been tellin' my grandmother how sad I was 'cause I knew I wadn' gettin' what I really wanted for Christmas, which was a puppy. My Dad wouldn't let me have a dog.

At that time he was buildin' up his business and he never had time to play with me. When he did get home, he was tired and irritated. I was an only child and I hadn't started to school yet. I was lonely a lot of the time.

When I stopped talkin', my grandmother studied my face for about a half a minute and then she said,
"Sonny boy, you're worried about what you want for yourself, an I can understand that, but Christmas is about givin'. Christmastime is when you think about makin' other people happy."
She picked up my hand off the quilt and held it in both her hands.
"That's when our Heavenly Father gave us the greatest gift of all. He gave us His own Son so that he could grow up and teach us about his Father, our Father - an about Love, about givin'... and bein' a help to one another.

"From the time he was a little boy, he was unselfish an good, an he cared about people whoever they were, an whatever shape they were in, an he always tried to be a help."

I wadn' seein' my grandmother sittin' on the edge of the bed, or my dad leanin' on the door frame and lookin' down at the floor. I was seein' the little boy, growin' an learnin', playin' around his neighborhood. Suddenly I had a thought.
"Granmaw, did the little boy have a dog?"
She smiled down at me.
"I don't know if he did or not, sonny."

She reached up an combed back my hair from my forehead with her fingers.

"But I know he went around doin' good all the time he was here. You might say his whole life was a gift to all of us. He taught us to be unselfish like our Father is."

She stood up then and said, "Now you go right to sleep. In the morning there'll be presents under the tree for everbody."

When she went out, my dad leaned around her to turn the light off. As I drifted down into sleep, I was thinkin' how that was the first time I'd ever seen tears in my dad's eyes. I wondered what was wrong.

A little later, I woke up for a few seconds when I heard my dad's car start up an drive down the driveway crunchin' the snow.

A strange sound woke me up the next mornin. At first I couldn't figure out what is was. I heard somethin' kind of like a baby cryin' only different, and then I heard a little bitty bark. By then I was goin' down the stairs full speed.

I'll never forget the scenes I experienced that mornin'. That little brown an black puppy, who I'd already named Beau, runnin' across the floor with a long wrappin' ribbon in his mouth, growlin' an barkin', pretendin' he was a big, mean, grown up dog. An my dad an me, playin' with a set of cars and trucks and a little green tractor I still have somewhere.

For the first time my dad was havin' fun at Christmas. It seemed like his eyes were rounder and his face wadn' so tight anymore.

Later, we built a snow man an Beau got all wet. Mom gave me a towel to wrap him up in. He went to sleep in my lap.

I didn't know at the time what had really happened to my Dad, I just knew it was a wonderful Christmas, and I loved everybody and everything.

(Hal Bynum, Andite Invasion/BMI From the Album The Promise 2002)

There'll Be Love

There'll be warm days and cold days
and spring days and fall days
There'll be sad days and glad days
and back-to-the-wall days
But always, and always, and always
There'll be love.

There'll be love in the morning
when the first rays of dawn
promise new life to the world,
As once again, you turn to me
with the innocence and shyness
you had as a girl.

We'll share our feelings and we'll share our fears
and walk in the sunlight of the unfolding years
In the bedrooms and the hallways
In large ways and small ways
and always, and always, and always
There'll be love

I promise you Love.

(Hal Bynum, Andite Invasion/BMI From the Album It's My Time 1995 and If I Could Do Anything 1998)

Winter Beaches

In the southern most reaches of sad winter beaches
where the umbrellas of summer
and the bright trappings of youthful romance
are replaced with lonely walkers
in heavy sweaters and long pants

Waves that have come all the way from Europe
disperse themselves silently on the cold lonely shores
Tiny bird-legged birds tirelessly continue
their cold, lonely chores
beneath the weak winter sunshine
that illuminates, but never warms.

My God, it seems like only yesterday
we held summer in our arms.

I walk the barren beach with
no spring in my step
in a body I've only been loaned
and I wonder how many seasons I have left.

(Hal Bynum, Andite Invasion/BMI From the Album The Promise 2002)